G000094831

A PRISONER IN RIO

BY THE SAME AUTHOR

Steven Berkoff's America

A PRISONER IN RIO

STEVEN BERKOFF

HUTCHINSON

London Sydney Auckland Johannesburg

Copyright © Steven Berkoff 1989

All rights reserved

This edition first published in 1989 by
Hutchinson

Century Hutchinson Ltd, Brookmount House,
62–65 Chandos Place, London WC2N 4NW

Century Hutchinson Australia (Pty) Ltd
20 Alfred Street, Milsons Point, Sydney, NSW 2061

Century Hutchinson New Zealand Limited
PO Box 40–086, Glenfield, Auckland 10, New Zealand

Century Hutchinson South Africa (Pty) Ltd
PO Box 337, Bergvlei, 2012 South Africa

British Library Cataloguing in Publication Data

Berkoff, Steven
  Brazil.
  1. Brazil. Description & travel
  I. Title
  918.1′0463

ISBN 0–09–174109–2

Phototypeset in Linotron Ehrhardt by
Input Typesetting Ltd, London
Printed and bound in Great Britain by
Butler and Tanner Ltd, Frome, Somerset.

Introduction

I was performing in my play 'Decadence' at the Wyndhams Theatre during the winter of 1987, when my agent rang to ask me if I fancied going to Brazil to act in a film based on the attempted and bungled kidnapping of Ronnie Biggs, who had scarpered to Brazil and was doing very nicely in Rio, much to the chagrin of British justice.

Brazil was one of those places I knew nothing about and would probably never have real cause to visit. It was as remote in my mind as China. But fortunately film thrusts you into some unexpected 'locales' and circumstances: one day you could be blearily shopping in Asda's supermarket, and the next you could be doing the samba in a congenial night spot in Rio, with all the pretence of a jaded jet-setter while tossing back *cachassis*, Brazil's lethal and delicious cocktail. You would sit outside in the warm balmy air at some midnight hour and cast your mind back to the dreary and unforgiving shores of Britain where 'Ye Grotty Pub' was throwing out its whining hordes at the ridiculous hour of 11pm. So I put my mind into a positive frame and read the script, which was your average adventure yarn, low on dialogue but heavy on local colour, macumba, samba and carnival. It was all there, with Biggs and I somehow threading our way through it. As I say, Brazil had not yet invaded my life except as a colourful Third World country which was hell-bent on destroying its rain forest. Then other images surfaced: of a Christ figure atop some clump of stone, a distant memory of that master-piece, *Black Orpheus* directed by Marcel Camus, and some classes in *capoeira*, a Brazilian fight/dance which I took in Camden many years before. I also had in mind a disturbing

5

and chilling documentary about the plight of a million children who sleep on the streets in Sao Paolo. So with these fragments in my mental album, I boarded the Pan Am flight that was (to save money) to take me the long way round to Rio. The director, Ledi Majewski, an ebullient Polish gentlemen, enthused about the script and about Jack Macfarland the character I was to play. My character was an uneasy fusion of two people, a Scotland Yard cop and a Scots mercenary. The resulting android was a bent Scottish cop! The plot revolved around the cop trying to illegally deport Biggs from Rio; he befriends him posing as a reporter and, being a Scotsman, frequently barks . . . 'Aye Ronnie' . . . I didn't spend too much time examining the concoction of a script that had obviously suffered from grievous bodily harm after too many hands hacking away at it. For me it was an adventure, and the director's enthusiasm was so encouraging that I didn't allow the warning signs (such as changing dates, expanding schedules and new scripts) to deter me. I started to get concerned when my flight path took me thousands of miles out of my route to save (understandably) cash, and I began to feel like a low-budget hack. I arrived and was whisked away to have my blood taken and my waste analysed, although my doctor's certificate was perfectly adequate for entering the shiny portals of L.A. I resented having a needle stuck in my arm to enter what I felt was a shanty town in the last stages of collapse. I eventually met a very charming raconteur called Ronnie Biggs to whom Lech introduced me with the words, 'He doesn't like the script, Ronnie.'

Ronnie Biggs smiled and gave me a warm strong handshake. I was rather surprised at how ordinarily decent and educated he seemed – how personable and responsible. Perhaps I had been expecting a retired villain with overtones of the 'Elephant and Castle', with the verbals leaking out from the side of his mouth. This man was articulate and professional, and was certainly no slouch when it came to making suggestions. The days passed and nothing much happened except for some 'impros' on the text. Eventually we did start and I found myself engaged in the biggest battle I've ever had with my conscience as to whether to pull the plug and leave. My fiftieth birthday coming up complicated matters with its traumatic number, and this was one of the reasons I saw the film as an opportunity to nurse my half century of life out of sight. In fact the next four months were mental and spiritual torture, relieved only by emptying my guts onto the following pages. I mean no-one any harm. I did find much warmth and charm in Brazil and its people friendly and good-hearted. My main accusation against the film was the crime of humiliation, both committed by me and against me. Me, for easy acceptance of something I did not really believe in and therefore should have refused, and the company for the maladroit way of dealing with the actors. As an actor I felt more and more aquiescent and a victim. It is the lot of us actors. The following pages are from my journal of my Brazilian adventure and how I dealt with it.

Steven Berkoff

Biggs Takes us to the Samba Hall
5 July 1987: day one

Actually ate a beautiful breakfast: small croissants, cheese and coffee; feeling at a loss being here and trying not to talk crap to the various nerds that surround film. Met Ronnie Biggs who was utterly charming and civilised and keen to tell us everything about his life which all sounded a great deal more interesting than what we have down in this script. Rio is fairly boring to my senses which have been pulverised by Acapulco, and I recognise the same grinding poverty, the kids selling the chiclets to you as you sit in the cafés, and the lean faces and the open palms of the poor young men condemned to Skid Row or trying to sell a map of Rio. This seems too obliterate initially any desire to see the 'sights', or even to be able to see the sights. The first thing you see, unless you are a tourist, is a human being like yourself, and his condition is what colours your mood. If you see a street of happy people, then you are happy, and if you see a café full of hungry, excited people then you are hungry and excited, and if you see desperate people begging you to buy something then I too feel desperate. It's not a complex, but contamination by mood.

Last night we all trouped off to a spectacle which was a kind of tourist's cabaret where you sit and watch on benches that wrap around the auditorium in a kind of horseshoe shape. You're allowed to bring in your plastic glass of *caiperena* and take pictures. The beauty of it is that you go up on the cable-cars, and when you get to the top the view is quite spectacular, even before you go in and see the show. Biggs entertains us on the way with tall stories and he seems to recall events with the clarity of a born raconteur, and supplies

8

names to all the small part players in the story as if it were
important to you or helped you visualise the character. I
suppose for him it's like putting studs or dowels into carpentry to help hold the thing together – Biggs is an ex-carpenter
and is as thorough in his speech as he is in his work, I have
no doubt. He tells us how Scotland Yard failed to extradite
him from Brazil and so, he feels, resorted to kidnapping him
by getting some 'heavies' to weasel him out of the country
and have him charged in Barbados which is under British
law. But there was a loophole discovered by his lawyer to do
with the fact that you cannot separate a father from his son,
and off he went Scot free! He recalls the events with great
glee as if it had just happened and not several years ago. He is
clean faced, non-smoking and fit looking, and communicates
enthusiasm for Brazilian Samba and music as his counterpart
in London or he himself might once have spoken about
football.

We arrive, and Biggs is already buying us drinks. We sit
and are blasted by the most awesome explosion of power I
certainly have ever witnessed in my life. A battery (aptly
named) of drummers playing with hands and sticks make a
deafening and thrilling cacophany of sound – not with mikes
and overloud speakers that ruin your eardrums for life, but
using the natural acoustics of the hall. The rhythm is stunning and your body immediately wishes to take off with it.
Only in Bali have I heard anything similar. This is lyrical,
powerful and African mixed with Indian Brazil.

The men seemed to stand with their drums hanging
around their necks. Their co-ordination is perfect. As if
sucked out of the air, beautiful female mulatto dancers are
drawn on by their sound. Voluptuous Rioccans tattoo the
floor with a display of Samba; each girl wrapped in tiny
shreds of cloth which only just cover the areas to give the
impression of one flowing fountain of flesh, and not broken
up by forests and hillocks. Their loins are covered in the
front by a whisper of sequined G-string which disappears
under their crutches, and the two great globes then fold over
the string as if it were not there. They carry themselves with

an air of sexual superiority, flaunting their strong lithe bodies
in front of the pale European audience, which is visibly awed
by this natural and basic presence.

And now they enter like birds of paradise, wearing costumes that are so dazzling and intricately made you can
barely believe what you have seen, before another costume
arrives, even more startling in its ambitions. Some have giant
tiaras and crowns, while others enter wearing colossal wings
attached to their bodies while still clad only in their tiny bits
of modesty. Multi-coloured feathers, attached to gigantic
silken capes, circle the stage proudly, and each seems to
improve on the one before and staggers the audience until
you believe there is nothing that they could not do – as
costumes come on that almost engulf the stage.

Now there are at least two or three dozen dancers on-
stage, plus the orchestra, and not much more than double
this in the audience – so one gets the impression of how
cheap labour must be. Behind these glittering, queenly costumes lie scruffy, tiny dressing rooms, and a poor mulatto
steps out of her butterfly wings and becomes a slightly scabby
(poor nutrition) young girl. But before this happens they will
have royally entertained an audience, and humiliated them
too, as they ask volunteers onto the stage to have an initiation
in 'Samba'.

One or two brave and unlikely candidates clamber up onto
the stage, staggering me with their sheer audacity to be able
to be made fools of and not give a damn – but then the joy
of being on stage and in the public eye for a few moments
must for them totally engulf any feeling of humiliation. I felt
it myself when a child at a T.V. show, since one feels, in a
sense, protected by the occasion. It's all so unreal. So these
Brits and Germans clamber up, and the beautiful underclad
mulatto with her svelte limbs and high heels shows a man a
few wavy movements from her well-articulated chassis which
looks as if it moves on ball bearings, and we all screech with
laughter as we see the man in his awful trousers and standard
clothes of mass-produced mediocrity attempt to emulate her.
What a laugh! *Quelle folie!* We almost like to be the sacrifice,

as if it were necessary to compensate them for years of brutal slavery and exploitation, so now we can be gently mocked by these sweet and docile people . . . Why not make utter assholes of ourselves for a few minutes as we try to mimic the strong supple movements of a young, beautiful half-black woman? Her life style has kept her thin and unspoiled and poor, and therefore able to dance really well, since it is the privilege of the poor to dance well, since that much is free. Let's be mocked and jeered since that will relieve us a mite of the guilt we feel when we see them in the street selling off their bodies. Of course they move well; they are black and sexy and beautiful, while the sins of consumerism have thickened our waists and stiffened our bodies and throttled our emotions. Maybe there's some truth in that.

7 July 1987

Spent the morning trying on costumes and Lech deliberating on the tie as if it was a great costume drama, or the tie contained the secret of Macfarland's personality. Also talks about pushing the film back another week and Peter Firth and I discuss the intractable script. Wandering around the supermarkets for the clothes: I am amazed at the affluence in one area and the desolate poverty in the other; and yet one thinks of supermarkets as democratic venues for both working and middle class. The shops are full of European styles, and the little cafés on most of the floors are marvels of invention and full of the most delicious things to nibble or gorge on. There is nothing like this in Britain – not that I have seen anyway – but you don't see many mulattos in the stores. The population of Brazil is huge anyway, so that even if only half are working it still gives you a sizeable consumer market. The rest subsist in squalor in favellas or shanties all over Brazil, so that an unemployment factor of 50%, which would cripple the welfare of most countries, hardly makes a dent here. Rather the opposite, since they provide an enormously cheap means of casual employment.

I changed rooms in the hotel, since the ones on the front

were noisy and I had the impression of great seediness and drabness. I arrived on a grey day and Rio was not at all as I expected. It only really looks good in the sun. Otherwise it seems to cower and be oppressive, and the poor sellers of T-shirts shelter under the awnings and ridiculously attempt to sell you a shirt as you pass, as if it was a mechanical action. It is just too painful to let a real tourist walk past without a try, even if it is cold and raining, and dutifully and pathetically they hold out a brief splash of colour as you speed by.

The hotel is surrounded by security guards back and front, armed with guns and walkie talkies, and they always try to look busy as you go past them, chatting furiously into their little machines to give an impression of industriousness and alertness. They are protecting the hotel against the poor downtrodden outside; or are they in fact only too aware that the poor don't always feel that downtrodden and may want a piece more of the action? So we are protected like a fortress, or like an armed camp. Nobody gets in without approval. The president, Sarny, has been in power for a few years during Brazil's symbolic return to civilian rule, but the army are never far away lest he get too concerned about the poor. Last week buses were turned over and set on fire in the main square of downtown Rio over a price increase of about two pence. My driver on the film tells me the average wage, or rather the minimum wage allowed now by law, is $40 per month! It doesn't seem possible to live since, while it is cheaper than England, it is not ridiculously cheap; so maybe he meant $40 per week – since Biggs tells me he pays his house boy $5 per day.*

The most relaxing and best part so far is to recline by the large pool and order wonderful cocktails called *caiperenas*, made from *cachassis*† and crushed limes, and eat in the balmy open air. The film has the makings of a turkey, or perhaps a chef's salad, with Brazilian and Swiss producers, Polish director, a script by an American, an English subject – Biggs of course – and me playing a Scots cop. But on the other

* I later learned that there is in fact a minimum wage of $40 per month.
† A lethal drink derived from sugar cane.

hand, it could have the makings of an exciting action pic against the background of the carnival in Rio, with thousands of erotically clad mulattos swinging their bums whilst we unfold our little tale. I think of *Black Orpheus*. It was one of the most exciting films of that period, and the tragedy is that the star of that film now plays a small part in this; as a baddy. He who was once so lithe and beautiful – and no one who saw him will forget him – now is a middle aged, paunchy, balding man with ten kids and a large waistline – but still he is blessed with the most beautiful smile in the world, which takes you back all those twenty-eight years. Film is such a strange medium, for here I am working with Breno, whom I admired all those years ago. Somehow you are allowed to penetrate the screen and find him still ensconced in Rio, and half expect him to get out his guitar and play until the sun rises – as did his muse Orpheus.

Paraguay

Next day we were flown to Paraguay in order to get entry visas to come back again. I'm finding all this a pain in my ass, since I had to fly via New York in order to use a free airline, which put six hours on the journey; mind you, it was a treat, but actors like to complain. And now we are shunted off to this god-forsaken place in Paraguay. I'm dragged out of bed at 5 a.m. and refuse to go. I want out. I've had enough and don't want any more of it. I'm even threatened with more blood and shit tests when I had already gone through this in Rio. I don't want to do this junk, let alone suffer the honour or privilege of doing it. But I am persuaded to go to the airport and reluctantly board a very strange plane that has problems with its wing flaps. The crew step out onto the wing and jump up and down until these are released. By this time I was sure that this is to be my end, and that it is on the cards that the series of events that culminated in my taking this job is to test my moral fibre and fitness to carry the torch for the world; that I have succumbed to money, temptation and ease, and the snuffing out of my life is a punishment meted out to those to whom God gives gifts which aren't used properly. He doesn't want to waste them further, and so will get rid of me and a few others in order to pass the muse on elsewhere. I am already mourning my demise and wondering if my last-minute will, made two days before I left, is in order, but at least I'm relieved that I had made it.

However we landed without incident and drove to a hotel on the river which links Brazil and Argentina. On the way I saw posters of a greasy looking character and imagined it was a 'WANTED FOR MURDER' poster, since the face was quite repellent, but I learned afterwards that it was the face of the Paraguayan dictator who had been in power for thirty-five years! – a tin-pot German governor called Stroessnor, who ruled by curfew, only recently lifted, and kept the country in peaceful slumberland and reasonably poor. We all wandered around the city after taking in the breathtaking view from the hotel of the river on the opposite bank. The city is called Asuncion, and we all drifted around like tourists, comparing the prices of Seiko watches like kids at a bazaar. And old station which looks as if it could have been one of the first from the gold rush days advertises trains to Buenos Aires. Steam trains! We pass an old café and wander in, since it looks suitably worn and low, like something out of *The Treasure of the Sierra Madre*. It's a kind of King's Cross area where the down and outs hang around. They're always attracted to stations since they are the exits and entrances of the body of the city, and obey nature's course exactly like the germs that fester around the human body's evacuating areas.

A man looking like Charles Manson's double keeps two monkeys in sacks and takes them out for show if he thinks he may have a customer. The poor monkey is tied by a piece of string round his throat and is hauled up by the idiot Manson-clone each time he wishes the monkey to sit on his lap. Then, having brutally demonstrated his mastery, he shoves the yelping creature back in the dark sack and ties the neck of the sack up. The monkey looks like a frightened victim. It is too close to human to ignore. Roberto Mann, our novice production manager who carries a big book on movie production around everywhere he goes, questions the man in Spanish, since he is trying to relieve our mutual discomfort and loathing. The man says he is selling the monkey. One feels like venting one's outrage on him, but Mark Slater, our young, suave New York producer, reminds us that we are aliens here and can do little except mildly protest. All poor countries must have something to enslave – even if it's a pathetic monkey that spent its life leaping through trees and now finds itself in a dark dirty sack. I thought we should buy the poor thing and set it free. The trouble is that he would only catch another and enslave that. The Manson double looks slightly insane, so we ignore him as he's beginning to rave at our criticisms.

We walked out, past a woman on the kerb selling raffle tickets to cars that were forced to slow down since there was a heavy flow of traffic outside the station. She was holding a young child in one arm and the raffle tickets in the other, and the child's fresh air was a nice juicy cocktail of carbon monoxide from the trucks and cars belching past. The child looks listless and just lets his head flop as the woman runs from window to window. You feel your spleen rise – if that's what it does – and the posters of this slob Stroessner seem to increase in number like Big Brother. After more exposure to the city, his expression seems, like a mask, to take on all the evil that exists. He now looks like the bloated murdering scumbag I first imagined in my ignorance when I arrived. In fact he looks like a pimp. There's been peace, a taxi driver says, for thirty-five years. A kind of slow, moribund dying I would have called it, and everywhere the military eye you suspiciously.

We drifted some more and ate some delicious *epinadas* – a kind of tasty Cornish pasty – and felt there was at least a semblance of normality. Next day we took a boat ride down the Paraguay river which is at least a mile wide: herons, vultures, and various exotic birds flitted on the opposite bank

and we were treated to an extraordinary display of a sunset
in a blaze of burning embers; and then it was black.

Friday 8 July

Last night wandered into the casino and overdid it as usual.
Was winning, but of course you keep on playing until the
odds are that you lose. That's the trick. If you left when flush
you'd be fine; but no, you play on and lose $20 for Peter
Firth. The faces in the casino – which is the only one in
Paraguay – tell you something about the country. Saw the
most disgusting creatures whose faces had scrawled on them
the only too visible corrupting effects of power without
restraint, plus total indulgence. Decayed and ruined, they
made George Grosz's impressions look positively flattering.
Soldiers manned the casino routinely, as if it was quite a
normal thing to have armed guards whenever there is the
slightest semblance of wealth. Bored, gun-toting soldiers with
giant bellies hanging over their belts as witness to their pay-
offs, stroll arrogantly around – and even in the quiet and
intense casino one sauntered up and down with his truncheon
flagrantly drawn. I would not like to imagine what these
bastards could perpetrate on any dissenters that they happened to lay their hands on; what unholy torture they would
easily be capable of – another country that the U.S.A. protects from the unspeakable terrors of 'Godless communism'.

The irony is that most of these people are devout Catholics
who see in Jesus's suffering a way of 'feeling', but have no
identification with his political beliefs. Blind devotion to
empty rituals and dumb ignorance of the words condemning
wealth, poverty, excess – as if one were to be obsessed with
Freud's death rather than with his ideas. The obsession with
Jesus as martyr is a way of de-fanging Jesus and making
ordinary people relate only to the dying, tortured soul with
nails in his hands and feet, not the fire and acid in his tongue.
Abetted by priests and all the clergy, they conveniently ignore
the social implications of his words, and worshipping a figure
in a state of agony, they identify with the agony and the

alleged perpetrators. This way of course is safe, and allows the greedy to prosper and still shed a tear at the agony. The Stations of the Cross and the scourging are totally irrelevant to the man himself and his ideas, and Jesus would be the first to vomit if he could see the disgusting world worshipping his torn and bleeding effigy, whilst allowing millions of children to sleep on the streets of Sao Paolo. However, the simple answer is that this vicarious purging through identification is less painful than giving away your money, which Jesus constantly demands. In fact closer examination of the words of the alleged Son of God might cause some degree of rebellion. One could also say that the spirit of Marx is far closer to Jesus than the spirit of Reagan or Thatcher – those constant twin spewers of godliness. If Jesus does return to this world he should avoid his biggest worshippers in South America. They might be tempted to kill him all over again.

Saturday 12 July
Back in Rio

Quite a good day yesterday, except for the worry about a small camera. I kept imagining 'opportunities' to use this and stared at second-hand and new ones. Walked past a few street people and their kids who sleep regularly on a particular stretch of pavement with their little brown heads sticking out under some old blanket. As I came back, one tiny brat was smoking in bed – he couldn't have been more than about six years old. I saw these children sleeping on bits of cardboard and I was tempted to believe that Sarny, the president, was an asshole.

Into breakfast comes an American invasion with their drony rich voices, slightly bored and laid back. I grab a table as far away as possible. They were not so bad but they just made too violent a contrast with what was lying just on the other side of the wall. So yesterday I walked through the antique market near the port which led to the junk market, with its boxes of old camera lenses staring like dead eyes, and broken-down electrical equipment. And then I kept walking to the main street, found myself facing some narrow streets, more like alley ways, bought some Samba music on cassette and found this restaurant which seemed to draw me in. Some restaurants do this. They have a worldly yet friendly look; they are inviting and yet sedate and look like they have been there a long time. The interior was wooden and brown, and the tables were covered in a white cloth and it felt good.

I sat and ordered, and meanwhile got chatting to an interesting-looking man with a beard at the next table. He turned out to be a German who was an expert on Indian languages and dialects! He was actually teaching the Mosquit Indians their own language which was in danger of being swept away – much like the *favellas*, the shanty towns that get washed away in the floods. He seemed so serene and learned that I was reluctant to answer his enquiry as to what I was doing in Rio, since my sordid fracas with the film world seemed so far away in ideals and meaning to what he was doing. However, when I told him he brightened up considerably and expressed great interest. He knew all about Biggs. Then an apparently English lady opposite, who had been throwing glances in our direction, came and joined me for a beer once the teacher had left. She told me she had been on a world tour and she had done this all alone. How brave, I thought – and I was thinking myself quite smart to have chosen this restaurant and that all my intuitions were right. She told me all the stories that one expects to hear – about the Indians, the countryside, the friendliness, the loneliness etc., and how she had husbanded her resources to the extent of returning to her hotel each night with two cakes for her supper, when she goes to bed to read and nibble her cakes. She says she had to read slowly so as not to get through too many books, since she can't afford to keep buying them. I had noticed her earlier when she ordered a beer and then another, which seemed a bit unusual, and when I offered her another she eagerly accepted. I thought she might have a drink problem until she told me she was an Ozzy, which helped to explain it somewhat – both her liberation and her booze tolerance.

We walked a bit through the town and had another drink

and she confessed her past life with some bloke that she married. He couldn't perform after a while, or got bored, and then they both went to a shrink who advised them what to do, which was to massage each other gently at least three times a week and wait for the feeling to return; but he kept forgetting to do it. She obviously needed to talk, and in fact lamented the few opportunities to do so in Rio. And then she related how the trip was paid for by selling her Dad's antique motor bike – called an 'Indian' – and went on to tell me all about the bike.

Meanwhile the table was approached by perfectly formed little brown faces clutching roses which they implored us to buy. The children were so beautiful and unspoiled – unlike their white counterparts – and will probably end up as adults pressing lift buttons in hotels. Our two white, moonlike faces attracted an assortment of objects being offered to us, and then an old guy threw down some transparent packets on the table which looked like clear shampoo but, on investigation, turned out to be tequila. Evidently the café didn't seem to mind that someone else was attempting to do its business, and accepted it as quite natural that others have to earn a living the best way they can, even if it overlaps with what the café sells. The waiters seemed human and helpful, struggling themselves to make a living, therefore understanding only too well the plight of others.

Then a few kids hovered around my shoes which obviously presented a pathway to riches. They sat on their little boxes waiting for the desire to reach me to have my trainers whitened. Meanwhile my Australian is getting more maudlin with each drink, and now wants to live in Peru near the Indians on a small farm she has heard about. Then an old man came selling caps, then more kids with wild roses, and mother with children with only hands out. Then a handsome young man with one leg cajoles my friend to buy a whirling light which makes patterns in the air.

As it grew dark we decided to explore a dance hall, and asked the waiter who recommended a place near Urca, which is near one of the beaches. The taxi dropped us off and we

joined a small queue of people at the box office. It felt good
to be queuing, like in the old days when I went to the Royal,
Tottenham, and you were full of expectancy for what the
night might bring. It could possibly change your life, which
certainly couldn't happen if you went to the pictures or to a
football match. At a dance hall there was the possibility of
mysteries unknown. So as we joined the queue a fleeting
semblance of that feeling came back. It wasn't like queuing
for the cinema where you'd get disgruntled, and anyway the
movie did it all for you. Here you are the author of your
experience.

And you could dance. There was this incredible sight of
at least two thousand people dancing; sitting at tables, eating,
drinking, walking about. The impact of the place hit me like
a thunderclap. The band was playing some gentle, jazzed-
up Samba and we were placed and served within minutes,
as if there weren't hundreds of tables there. We didn't have
to wait long for the drink either. The faces at the tables were
simple, normal, pleasantly happy, released, at ease – no yobs
marauding up and down, no bad vibes or tension; just people
gently holding each other closely as they danced to a slow
Samba.

The band was good and didn't stop playing, and I thought
of the lousy 'Nite Spots' in London where desperation for a
dance and a jig had led me, and the disgusting creeps I used
to see there. And here people were laughing and enjoying
themselves, eating and drinking and of all ages. Middle aged
men with their wives, for whom this might be a regular
Sunday jaunt – no one did any picking up since most people
seemed to know each other or came in groups.

After an awkward start it was a good day. The girl went
home after the dance since she was into drinking and I was
tired. We split up, a bit disillusioned with each other. But at
least two people were able to enjoy talking and seeing Rio
in a way that wouldn't have been possible alone. And I was
grateful to her. I hope she finds happiness in Peru.

Scotland versus England
14 July

The director's driving me mad as to whether I play my role as Scots or English, having discussed the character's 'Glaswegian' image for two months. MacFarland has been written as a Scots mercenary-come-cop who leads the kidnappers and so I've been working on my Glasgow accent which is nay bad after a stint at the renowned Citizens Theatre in the sixties. The Citizens Theatre was a sanctuary in the hell-hole of the crumbling Gorbals slums where I had ample opportunity to absorb the sound of the place. So, armed with a reasonable impersonation of a jock, I plunged in, regurgitating memories of every Scotsman I met or heard, from Billy Connolly to the butcher next door to the theatre who sold me a cut called 'Popes-eye steak' which I'd fry to a treat in ma wee digs. Happy days!

But now after the first day's shoot the director gets cold feet about the accent and thinks I should 'try it "London" . . . ' My character was about to be demolished into a thousand pieces. How vulnerable actors are to the whims of the director. What a toe-rag some directors can make you feel. I was tempted to tell him to find someone else. It's not just the difference in a dialect, since the whole of one's being is involved. London and Glaswegian are completely different species of animal from one other. The body language, down to the very armature of muscles in the face, are different, and so it's not just a question of voice. 'Play it English,' he snorts, after a whole days shooting. 'No way laddie,' I say. 'It makes utter nonsense of the whole character and the way it's written in the script. . . ' We continue our argument under the shadow of the stone Jesus on top of Corcovado,

21

whose open arms embraced the suffering of all below. Eventually we compromise on the accent (which reduced its caustic efficiency) and since my suit fits so badly I decide to be resourceful and play the character as a bollock-scratching sleaze. Biggs tells me that the character my part is based on used to kick a football round his hotel room using the open wardrobe as goal. Naturally this juicy morsel is not in the script, since my character is a factoid between two real people and thus is neither.

I hate having to deal with inflexible and dogmatic people who claim at the outset that a cooperative spirit will prevail until you find yourself at the end of a confrontation over each suggestion you make that might ease the pain. Those words are mighty hard to swallow. Why is film dialogue inevitably so shitty, so lacking in imagery, wit, or metaphor? It has to be 'real' and identifiable to the mass stony audience that will swallow it, as long as it's coated with a few visuals. So I decide on a lighter Scots accent. But if I did play it as a Londoner, I mused, I could also bring elements of my past to that. But then Biggs is played as a Londoner by Paul Freeman and a contrast has to be established between the two protagonists – which is emphatic in the script, written in part by Biggs himself before it was altered.

So I go backwards and forwards. Suddenly I am sick of the whole thing and regard it as a waste of my life. I start to regret not leaving at the beginning, since each day's film in the can is a further tightening of the noose. You can't leave now. So we stick to a 'light' Scots. It sounds O.K.

Shot scene today driving round and round a rare old slum downtown. A man was picking bits of chicken out of a rubbish dump covered in flies and the collected refuse of the neighbourhood. The crew were anxious to catch this and did. The man was totally impervious to the camera poking its long nose into his plight. What was so shocking about the scene was its normality. Nobody in the street paid any attention and some kids kicked a ball around the hot dry street while the man – who looked quite fit – stood legs apart and straddled possessively over his filthy rubbish heap. The doorways starting to fill with families who came to watch as the camera chose their filth and wretchedness to decorate the film. Every doorway was crammed with kids of all ages, some holding in their arms their newly arrived brothers and sisters while hardly out of the womb themselves. It was an adventure in the street. While looking desperately poor they showed no sign of dirt on their clothes, and their little shorts were clean. They had not lost pride in themselves. One girl was helping beautify her friend's frizzy hair by putting it into curlers. They are mostly all black or mulatto round here and seem to have perfectly formed lithe young bodies and perfect moonlike faces with strong teeth and fine features. But the women seem to grow gigantic asses as they get older, perhaps because they don't play football all day like the boys.

The other street people seem to have no home except the pavement, and one man with a broken leg was living in a kind of wheelbarrow which also served as his bed. I've seen quite a few of these barrow homes now, so they must be quite a thing to get hold of since you can wheel your house around when it rains. With a cardboard bed you'd have to carry your stuff on your back. There was an utter helplessness among these less fortunate slum-dwellers with no hope and nowhere to go. Nothing to do. However in Britain you are forced at least to fight for your Social Security or turn up in the welfare offices. Something to look forward to each week, if only the money order and the sense that you are protected and the state won't let you die. Also in Britain I believe the ordinary man in the street does care about his fellow man, and sometimes cares passionately. But here the attitude is one of supreme indifference. There is no welfare, no social security, no help from the state. This here is the end of the world: no concern; no net to care for those who have fallen by the wayside. Here the street is as far as you can fall, the stone pavement your eternal resting place. Your rights are as much as your open palm can hope to draw from the passing public. Here the garbage heap is your welfare and the poor educational system makes sure that many more will end up on it. And religious bigotry will emphasise the desperation as babies drop regularly with no hope for their future, except begging or selling peanuts on the Copacabana. If they are young and cute, for a while they will soften a tourist's heart. But eventually they may fall ill or receive an infection from walking about so often with no shoes, and they have neither the will nor the knowledge to get treatment. They will wait until their foot must be amputated at one of the few 'poor' hospitals.

Giant jewellery shops line the Copacabana in an almost obscene display of profligate riches; and the city boasts giant shopping malls so there is a massive division of wealth. Most employers stick to the level of minimum wages ($10 per week). There seems to be an awful lot of German industry here which, while pouring lots of plant and capital into the country, has a captive and low paid work force. They seem to be everywhere. They even have a German town called Freiborg!

In Rio one is not at all ashamed to be wealthy and display it. The yellow faces can be seen gorging themselves in the beach cafés, and who worries about the poor in the slums? In one sense, by doing nothing for them you deny the problem exists. Once you acknowledge the poor by allowing them a piece of the cake, they have rights and can demand a slightly bigger slice. Why not? We create the poor. Best ignore them, leave them to rot in their slums and distract them with a carnival once a year.

We wrap up filming for the day and have made a small contact with the families in the street. We fool around and even have some pics taken with them. They seem very happy to have had us there and there is not the slightest element of resentment. The dung heap has been picked clean and the local tavern on the corner is filling up. Their gin is the familiar *cachassis* and is very potent at about 20 pence a glass. At least forgetfulness is cheap.

The Actor's Life
20 July 1987

The actor's life in film, contrary to all beliefs, is a hard one. For me it's even more hard, since in the past I've been responsible for the words I say and the actions I perform. When I come back to earth, so to speak, I am always amazed at what has been going on in my absence after doing 'real' work. Coming down to earth, I have to mouth the trivialities of the movies like an humble marrionette. I can think of no work in the creative media more passive than being an actor on film. If lucky, you are plucked out of your home and ensconced – sometimes first class, with champagne poured down your throat – in a plane bound for territory you would never normally be inclined to travel to. You are constantly referring to your agent to be on the alert for any cheating going on, or any failure to accord you a separate trailer and not a shared one, and, of course, for a separate card on the credits. I protested that I couldn't care less if I wasn't even on the credits, but this is considered the naiveté of the neophyte. Soon, they prophesy, you will be as obsessed by the size of your name on the screen as they are, and you will have sleepless nights wondering if they are going to cut your scene, and sweating over whether you will be asked to do the scene nude; fearing the confrontation between your principles and somebody's interpretation of them will be seen as masking your alleged prudishness, whereas it is their artlessness which is the culprit.

Unlike nurses, engineers, teachers, carpenters, oil drillers and divers, who actually control their own work – be it only a part of the whole – the actor has little say in what he does or how he does it; or what he says. Nor does he wish to. He

will be guided to his hotel like some precious robot, where
he is likely to rhapsodise on the view, or lack of it. Then he
speedily repairs to the bar to get drunk with his colleagues,
who are already 'wised up' to the situation and saving heavily
on their *per diems* by getting the early breakfast – 'since you're
billed with the crew and not separately' – even if it does
mean getting up at 7 a.m. They have already sussed out the
good restaurants, which are revealed with great seriousness
– as if they have uncovered the tomb of Tutenkhamen. They
tend to stare at you and rave about the 'sea food' . . . and
'last night's blow-out' . . . 'The prawns were *ay . . . may . . .
zing!*'

The sheer passivity, allowing no involvement in the creation of the film either in writing, locations, costume – 'That
tie looks terrible on him . . . 'aven't you got something
else?' . . . You stand there, having been demoted instantly to
the third person, while an intense wardrobe man flings ties
around your neck and the director squeezes his eyes up or
even cups his hands together to form a small rectangle in
impersonation of a lens. You are rarely consulted – it's as if
this is the first time in your life that you have worn clothes;
whereas your taste, instinct for colour, and total familiarity
with yourself should be far more creative than anything an
outsider could consider. However, you are not meant to have
a mind, and so you wear the most appalling shirt you have
ever worn in your life which is not only ill-fitting and looks
like a sack of turds but makes *you* look like a sack of turds.
The shirt is evil and the tie malevolent. Nothing matches or
has any cool or style.

In the theatre of course the actor's involvement with the
director starts from the first day and will affect the play's
success, so that an inventive team of actors will improvise on
a bad text until the right button is pressed and the thing jells
– for which they will receive no credit but the satisfaction of
having made it work. A clever director will aggregate the
resources of a complex group of people who are your cast,
and use it, whereas a duller director, unable to cope with the
wide range available of experience and complexity, would

rather keep that particular tap tightened. He will invent the moves for you, decide on the clothes, the text, and how you act – since he may have read something about the *auteur* . . . or read the work notes on *Citizen Kane*.

Here on location the actor's only relief – unless he is playing a great leading role and feels 'expressed' – is to enjoy food'ndrink'ncrumpet. He becomes a slave, released for the night in the hope that he will not get too pissed for the next morning's work. And if he does, it becomes an ever-growing legend about how much he drank and what he said and how long he has been pissed. The legends of pissed actors have been dined out on for years, as if this was some kind of great achievement of will, rather than one of hopeless and pathetic weakness. Eventually the same clods will achieve great notoriety when they get off the booze and tell the world of their achievement in the same breathlessness as a man telling how he climbed Everest.

Usually the hairdressers and make-up people stick together as a clique and wax on every day about how marvellous Liz Taylor was to work with, and how sweet this one was, and what a gentleman he was, and what a lady she was . . . and on and on, since their lives are totally dominated by how 'nice' and 'pleasant' the stars are to them. They are most willing to give you a bad epitaph if you don't watch out. When not bad-mouthing someone or unduly genuflecting to someone else, they tend to talk about their property in Sussex and little summer villas in Spain; or their dogs; or both.

The actor arrives and, in his excitement, may booze too much on the first night – feeling a bit alienated to find himself one minute in Camden Town and the next in Acapulco or Zimbabwe, and perhaps having departed on a bad note having rowed with the missus. So he mulls over it in Acapulco and fails to get through on the blower, and gets well and truly in the hotel bar with the other actors exchanging stories about pissed actors and 'When I worked with Peter O'Toole'. Everyone will fight to buy the round, since actors are very sociable and don't want to give the impression of meanness as they're going to be together for several weeks. He is likely to insist on getting the next round, even if he is dying for his sleep and jet-lagged as well as pissed.

The next day he arrives on the set in a state of reverence for the text, and the director and he might get into a corner to decide if the actor should say 'and' instead of 'if'. The actor will be subdued by the overwhelming activity of the set – the elex, rigs, props, cameras etc., and look hopefully around for the tea trolley to bring some tasteless horse piss – if you happen to be in Pinewood Studios. He will see tracks being laid for cameras to fly along, mounted by cameramen whose necks are weighed down by the apparatus of the craftsman: his filters, lens and viewfinder – the genius of the mechanical world which the lighting man must master. The humble actor either takes all this in and tries not to be fased by the complex science of movies and view his role as a necessary and vital part ... or he will resist being over- whelmed by it all and the superior technical knowledge of the cinematographer, and tell jokes about the events of the night before, and mug through his lines. He is called to rehearse and somehow is moved about here and there – whatever you do, try and step on the chalk line or you're bloody out of focus. That's the main thing: hit your marks! The make-up comes and sticks a little bib under your chin so as not to soil you and make you feel like a tiny tot once again.

The actor rehearses now for the take. The lines are usually incredibly banal, since not all films are *Mephisto* or *Citizen Kane*. Usually they are clichés piled on cliché. The actor sits there without flinching. He knows; he has worked in the theatre and knows about good dialogue and resonant text. Even a modest actor would have done, in rep, a Chekov or two, plus an Ibsen, a Miller, or a Strindberg, and one or two Williams – both Tennessee and Emlyn. So the actor will know when he is putting garbage into his head. Now you see why Burton went down the plughole and that people brought up in the land of Dylan Thomas and not Bob Dylan couldn't face the sheer torture of the drivel they were poisoning their minds with. So they escaped to the boozer to wash it away; or at least try to.

So the actor sits there and dumbly contemplates the text. A nurse would certainly question her equipment if she felt it not suitable to the expression of her skills, as would an engineer his tools, a draughtsman his apparatus and a teacher his books; even a tailor his shears. But here a group of highly intelligent and experienced actors become like lobotomised robots, swallow the words, poison their brains with them, and spew them out just as they are written. They have no interest in changing them since, unlike in the theatre, the words can't be 'tested' in front of an audience over a few tryout weeks on tour. There is not much point in doing more than some touching-up if you are allowed or your advice is sought. The only interest is the 'Silly Money' – as they are fond of calling it – at the end. 'That's O.K. We'll shoot that' . . . 'See you in the bar luv. . . .'

Tuesday 21 July
Lord Jim

Had drinks with Ronnie B. in the Lord Jim pub last Sunday. It was a warm afternoon and what made the pub different from most was the opening hours from lunch time to 1 a.m. – and children welcome. Of course being in Rio did help, but it was the 'Children Welcome' that made the difference since no other Rioccan bar or café would need to say that since it is taken for granted that kids are part of your life. So the owner revealing the terrible truth about his past and the British way of death in its gormless pubs advertises 'Children Welcome' as if he had to warn people that this wasn't England and those laws don't apply – even if it is a pub. The gates are open; no restrictions; no repressions; no guzzling up at a harshly called 'time'. . . just a few people having lunch and a drink on a Sunday afternoon, chatting quietly, enjoying a piece of nostalgia without the pain; and 'Children Welcome' – a nice sign.

Carnival

Rio doesn't much remind me of Carmen Miranda but as I
said, it does bring back vividly one of the greatest movies
of the fifties: *Black Orpheus* – Marcel Camus' stunning re-
interpretation of the Orpheus legend set in the time of the
carnival. The carnival permeates everything here and is the
dominant factor that explodes all over the city in February
when the streets are seething with music and colour and
bare-assed, wriggling damsels. The pavements will be
thronged with tourists of every nation on earth and they will
mutually bake under 100° of wet heat. Thousands of normal
men and women will go insane for one week and, wearing the
most outrageous, outlandish and bizarre costumes imaginable
they will rid themselves of centuries of 'civilising' and conditioning and become what they imagine their true hearts to
be: their real inner selves. British football fans work all week
in offices and factories and for the big foreign matches turn
into a crowd of violent lunatics, venting hatred and bottled
up repression that they hardly suspect they have, but which
they truly have absorbed in Britain. And what comes out is
their loathing. I suppose miners who come out of the pits
cough up coal dust. It's the conditions which create the
disease. But in the same way, in Brazil, what comes out is
the people's fantasy, since they are hardly repressed the rest
of the year – except economically. What exudes from them
at festival time is wealth: wealth of colour, costume, sex and
dance. To be crazy. To be free after years of slavery.

The Samba, which seems part Indian, part African and
some parts Jazz, will express the nation in a riotous orgy of
freedom of expression when all the arts seem to come together in the biggest carnival the world has seen. Costumes in
the shapes of animals and birds, wigs from the courts of
Charles Ludwig, bizarrely transposed to Brazil; creations so
dazzling that they seem to have been created in dreams. The
Samba schools are organisations rather like football clubs
with thousands of members, and each member takes on one
costume and may spend the year designing it and sewing it

with the help of his family and adding more and more bits
– and it has to fit with the associations of colour and theme
which would be decided early. Then, in the final day of the
carnival, each team parades in the great stadium and the
victor is decided. It's a freedom that costs nothing but gives
everyone something, even if it dulls the grinding poverty of
the favellas and so quells the people's desire for revolution.
It's non-violent, sexual, physical, musical and insane. But it
is also happy! What do *we* have? New Year perhaps, which
after a drunken Xmas is merely an aftermath ... But for
real passion we do have the Heysel football riots.

La Scala: Night Shoot

Filmed at La Scala and our director – totally obsessed with
the visual – photographed endlessly – and I mean endlessly
– a chorus line of dancers – stunning, long-legged mulattos
whose grandparents were probably slaves and would be
thrilled to see how far their daughters had come, adorned in
feathers and wearing bits of diamanté between their thighs.
The cameraman, George Moradian, weaved up and down,
holding the camera and using it like a paintbrush – or a giant
mouth, sucking it all in. Both men in fact were like kids at
a picnic, disbelieving their good luck – all this flesh and for
next to nothing, maybe dancing all day for twenty dollars. So
they gorged themselves sick on their feast, on their flesh
mountains, while the actors waited, and waited ... and
waited ... and ... waited ... and waited.

Then on came a really brilliant dancer, who performed a
solo piece, beating a small thin drum he used as a wheel and
juggling with it, he performed really incredible feats ...
again ... and again ... and again. Surely, I thought, they
must have the shot by now. The man was getting tired and
I felt for him since he put everything into each take. But this
was a feast for drunks, and they supped.

So we waited for our little scene, which was to be the real
reason we are here today, and the background of the Samba
hall is the thinnest excuse to take advantage of 'Samba'. We

meet Biggs in the most unlikely setting of the Samba hall so
that we may graze the lens with all these extraordinary
goings-on before our feeble scene is unfolded. By contrast
to the events preceding it, it feels like a wet fart.

Asses, crotches and tits are fed into the machine until 4
a.m., when some wilted, disgruntled and bored actors were
finally led to their marks; whereupon the worst acting ever
to be put on film was greeted by the director as 'Beautiful',
since there was nothing he could say except try lamely to
relieve the torture. The actors tried to mouth their wooden
dialogue with difficulty, however, the Dunkirk spirit prevailed
and some attempt was made to do 'something with it'. At
this time I was having trouble remembering my lines and
even the rewrites I was attempting to enliven them with.
After a while – as must inevitably happen, since a surfeit of
the sweetest things the deepest loathing to the stomach brings
– the sexy mulattos became less and less sexy and their bums
became simply what you sit on the loo with. The sweaty
jockstraps and G-strings start to take on other, less welcoming, images. I recall a friend who danced with Nureyev, and
we discussed the mixture of shit and high culture, and how
that beautiful gilded prince in his immaculate white leotards
left behind the most exquisitely coated jockstraps. Quite
natural in the circumstances – but something we don't
ponder until these asses and crotches are shoved down our
throats.

The girls thankfully left, and another, fresher group came
in. The union leaders demanded another 1,000 cruzeiros
($18) and there was a bit of debate and frowning at this
exorbitant sum, but it was finally agreed and we got on with
more tits and ass. I am instructed not to overdo the Samba
or make it funny, but a Scotsman at large in Rio would be
precisely rather stupid-looking I would have thought, and
that was the whole point. 'Biggs' is guiding me around the
fleshpots of Rio and humiliating me as I drag my Scots
uptightness over the proceedings. Thus, like a ship being
guided in over the rocks, I should fall apart. However the
film really is a fiction on the life of Biggs, and the word

'fiction' allows a writer to perpetrate whatever sins he wishes since it is not meant really to be an accurate portrayal of the events – which I think is a great shame, since this amalgam of Biggs doesn't constitute his character one bit. And Biggs himself is quite fascinating enough without embroidery or fictionalising. It is as if his character got in the way of the drama.

Obsession
Friday 24 July

Should have left the first day. This person is unbelievable in the way he wastes actors. Again, I'm driving around relentlessly, and that's all we seem able to accomplish. I'm surprised I ever considered this, or writing about it rather than fleeing. We're not dogs and some kind of creative attitude is necessary. I feel humiliated, disgusted and jaded. I wish I had stayed in bed rather than going to Paraguay for the stupid work permits. What a humiliating end to my fiftieth year . . . What a disgrace.

Thanks to P.F. I broke this mood with a Samba lesson, since he is obliged to have them for a sequence in the film and it must be a big bore to do it alone, and so I provided at least a bit of company. Miguel, who is a mulatto and a skilled dancer, took us through our paces. We leapt up and down the hotel room. The movements were not too difficult and it took me out of my introspective gloom. I am obsessed to distraction about buying a small pocket camera – the kind that costs £50 and you whip out at parties or in the street. My giant zoom lens is too big to take out casually and I imagine all sorts of 'photo opportunities' when a little built-in flash would be perfect. So get it! But for some unknown reason it sticks in my throat.

I walk back and forwards up and down the Avenida Copacabana staring at the little thing in the camera shop, and it would seem that it has lodged itself into my heaven and hell syndrome. As if the solution one way or the other gives peace and tranquility; or torment – but since I am in torment now the only thing to do would be to get it. I feel as if I am on the rack. It can't mean so much. I refuse to believe it. All

34

day I stare at Mark's little smart Olympus and start to envy him for it . . . I think about the British actors I have worked with in the past who seemed so free on the set and off it, but were dead in front of the cameras and I comfort myself that I should be worried about trivia when I have a power and flow, feelings and skills to my work. I numb myself to distraction. Crazy fool. There is so much here that passes you by because of your stupid and petty fears that cripple you. Look at the poor woman sleeping behind the cardboard. Is not such a thing shocking – and you should record this horror.

Later: So I rush like a moron to stare at the camera in the window while making moral evaluations, but couldn't decide, spun on my heel and went guiltily to work, passing the figures condemned for life to their pieces of cardboard. Drove again today, round and round and ended up on the beach in Urca. Became incensed at watching the director continually prodding a beautiful caged bird, over and over again to get it to 'react'. In the end I got Helmut to buy the camera and described it and the shop where I examined it. Start behaving like a movie actor and sending the boy out to get things! 'Hey take these ulcer pills round to Ronnie Biggs will you.' Helmut my driver whizzes off, glad not to be hanging around all day. He is a sensitive youth and already confesses he dislikes the tense atmosphere on the set. So he brings it back, all new-looking and black, and I take some pics immediately to justify it. I heard Peter Firth getting obsessed about a cassette deck. He wants a 'powerful' one. It's the same bloody syndrome. You go away and feel lonely and start trying to make a home away from home. I quite felt for him then.

The Cardboard People

24 July 1987

Felt a great deal better after some human contact in the shape of Biggs, on my way back I contrasted my petty obsessions that had me the previous day running around comparing cameras with the poor and miserable curling up for the night with their babies inside their cardboard boxes. The children take this for granted as children do who know no better or worse. For them it's quite normal to sleep on a piece of cardboard, inhaling the traffic fumes and watching the people pass by. The only solid wall they have is the one they lean against. A whole family who live and sleep this way – sometimes standing a piece of card on its side to make a kind of low fence. It's better here. At least you can be seen and others who are not quite so poor might throw in a few pennies or even a sandwich.

One day I saw an overweight Swiss or German hand over half of the sandwich she was eating to an old lady who took it quite eagerly. I was just walking behind her since I was getting familiar with the area and even with the shanty squatters whom I had photographed in exchange for a small remittance. I was smiling because the girl had an attitude which was almost beatific as she handed over half of her cruddy sandwich, which would have only made her fatter than she was. She wasn't fat in that loose way that mothers sometimes are, or plump girls. She had that kind of tight, bursting fatness from greed and little sex. She saw me smiling and I said, 'Good for you' – and actually meant it since at least it was a gesture in the right direction. She mistook my meaning I think, and then, in a most holier-than-thou manner, said that more people should give something to these poor people, looking at me as if her pathetic example of beneficence should have set me on fire. I wanted to tell her to sod off but was too stunned by how moved she was that she almost crapped.

However the street squatters were quite unmoved by anything. They accept it as a fact of life that you don't brush your teeth in the morning, or sit peacefully on a toilet seat, or sprawl over a nice kitchen table while Mummy gets you your porridge and you watch Pinky and Perky or other rabid shit that children are supposed to love, or fight over who gets the first bath or the best toys at Xmas. There are plenty of poor in Thatcher's Britain too, but here you know they have no chance. In Britain one day the herd will lift their heads from *EastEnders* and *Sunday Night at the London Palladium* and see what a slum the country has become and hopefully they'll wake up and kick the bitch into kingdom come, and all the rot that goes with her. But here there is no such chance. The cancer is here to stay. There is the merest illusion of voting, but the power is in the hands of the few with the shadow of the military hovering nearby. The rich get richer and the poor die.

When you see these sad little figures with their small, sleeping faces, it makes for bad comparisons. Even reading *The Sunday Times* become odious, seeing how everyone is crowing about themselves and their stupid and vain lifestyles. The pomposity of it all. There is something about *The Sunday Times* and its reflection, or the way it chooses to reflect Britain that is both charming and distinctly repulsive. The S.T. makes me feel as if the country had been glazed over in some gelatinous substance where daylight rarely penetrates. I greedily leapt on the paper for a long read of what's happening in the old sod, and read it from cover to cover. What comes across is an insufferable smugness and an almost cosy infantilism, worn as a badge of liberation . . . 'Books for those long wet Summer afternoons' . . . and the junk that was so carefully chosen. Under their jelly they wax about 'Glowing Amber Beers' and 'Roly-Poly Puddings' . . . I suppose in England it all sounds so winsome and cute. But from here it makes you go . . . *uuuuuuuugh!*

Biggs

25 July

Biggs is O.K. Lives in a charming old house in an old preserved part of Rio called Santa Teresa. You could if you liked get there by an ancient rickety tram for the equivalent of one penny. It careers around corners with its human cargo bursting out and clinging to the sides: a good symbol of Rio. Biggs tells me they all signed a petition to save the two trams from the knacker's yard, so one has the feeling he is part of a responsible community spirit. He is proud of his flat which is really part of a large house with a stunning view over the city and is cooler than the furnace down there when the summer really comes. He's done the place up by himself and has the best carpentry I've seen in years, made up by a local carpenter to his specifications. 'Fancy getting the old nosebag on', he says as we play some snooker on a mini-table in his back room. 'How's that?' I query. 'Dinner, mate. Fancy some grub down the road' . . . and we head for a *churascurio*, which is not so much your familiar steakhouse but a charnel house which serves the needs of the most slavish devotees of red flesh.

We sit in a favourite place and swiftly knock back two *caiperinas*, which are the standard cocktail of Brazil. A large dollop of liquid fire derived from sugar cane and crushed limes with sugar stirred in; over loads of ice. It hits you immediately and tastes good, the lime and the sugar deceiving you into its real knock-out power. The waiter comes at you within no time with barbecued sizzling meat on a skewer and with a lethally sharp knife shaves off a slice at your table. And as he slices it you hold one end with your fork to prevent it unseemlily slapping onto your plate. 'Cheers Ronnie.'

'Cheers to you and a toast to . . . what?' '*Prisoner of Rio*', I suggest. 'Nice one. Right . . . to *The Prisoner of Rio*.

Ronnie looks well for his years, like a lascivious satyr, silver hair curling round the base of his neck and blue laughing eyes that have a habit of fixing you with quite an intent and scrutinising glare; but then he covers up his scrutiny immediately with an easy flow of continuous jokes. He's a very friendly bloke, looking at home here, just like a wandering Odysseus who would be at home anywhere. He translates the Portuguese menu with great expertise and we order some more drink – '*Dois mas caiperina por favor*' – in good cockney. He liked Australia and had a good time there until his cover was blown when a picture of him appeared in a local paper and he legged it to Rio. He gives me a brilliant description of his escape from the Scrubs which ended with 'paying two mates £500 each to hold the two screws down while I nipped over.' He tells me about the plastic surgery which not only altered his features but at the same time seems as a bonus to have rendered him more youthful. Now he's quite a ladies' man, even if he has to shave behind the ears.

He relishes telling me the story of his breakout as if for the first time, and it's not only fascinating but well told, in the way only a real working class urban villain could. He holds you in the palm of his hand, and it's an act he's perfected since he now regales tourists with it. He's one of the attractions of Rio after the Sugar Loaf and the Christ at Cocorvado, that giant figure thrust into the sky which is as much Rio's signature as Big Ben is ours. The tourists' guide books him for a few jars and a chat, and then Biggs sells them signed T-shirts printed with I WENT TO RIO AND MET RONNIE BIGGS, HONEST! signed by Biggs himself. Tourists will fall over themselves to pay ten dollars to have the privilege of meeting the last of the Great Train Robbers. He's almost a Grand Seigneur now; a regal figure that holds his six feet two inches very proudly for someone approaching their sixtieth next birthday, and runs up the stairs outside his flat two at a time because it's too depressing to contemplate the long staircase otherwise. It's his workout.

He still has powerful arms and shoulders from years of carpentry and I quite believe it could have taken three men to hold him down during the abortive kidnap attempt carried out by 'mercenaries' in 1981. Since Slipper of the Yard failed some years earlier the attempt was up for grabs, although Ronnie entertains the idea that the Yard were behind it.

So the film *Prisoner of Rio* is loosely based on that. Loosely, since for some reason the two separate events are merged and fictionalised slightly to allow the director some imaginative 'action' – and that is to shoot it all with the yearly bacchanalian carnival as a background. In the end the script becomes a struggle between the life styles of two men, one of whom succumbs to the pull of Brazil etc., etc. And that one is me. So the 'writers' have overlaid the script with some ornate action and odd philosophising, plus some pretty strange dialogue, while the story Biggs is telling me is simply rivetting. 'Biggsy', as most people call him, is not too happy with the script but as a kind of sporting bloke doesn't fuss too much and hopes for a good outcome. I myself fail to understand why people can change a perfectly good yarn for some hokum. But that is the nature of people who film the people who live.

Biggs, like many of his ilk, is a person we flippantly refer to as streetwise. This hackneyed expression is now used to describe any greedy opportunist. However streetwise implies a certain rough ethic or unwritten code of laws in which society moves. A streetwise person will obey a system of laws which have a definite and indisputable morality to them, and survival often depends on a healthy adherence to them. It is having a nose for the fake. It is also a survival code in prison where alleviating common suffering depends on a certain fraternity and where men will do time rather than 'spill' on their colleagues; except for informers of course. So if someone like Biggs expresses doubts about some elements of the script then a producer who fails to listen does so at his own peril. After all, it comes from the horse's mouth. He was there. But the film world has a law of its own and much of that is governed by the alleged audience's taste, and the desire to appease the taste rather than introduce it to new flavours. The risk is too high.

However Biggs is stoical about the whole thing and wants it to succeed. 'I'm on points', he says. I didn't think of asking him if he had any train money left but the betting is that he's gone through it, or most of what was left. The film will no doubt be an excellent action caper with Biggs somehow traced in but not as the vital three dimensional figure that he is.

Outside on Biggs's veranda his parrot screeches and the dogs wrestle with each other. It's a cosy set up and his smart son swears efficiently in English and Portuguese. The parrot is a large beautiful bird that has obviously received a lot of grooming and attention, and Biggs plays with it like a toy. The bird is totally trusting and feels safe with him. Biggs thrashes me for the fifth time on the billiard table, since he is familiar with all the grooves on it. 'Does the parrot ever fly off?' I ask, since it's left on a perch on the terrace and is not restrained by anything. 'Oh yes, every few months he goes on a fly-about'. 'Of course he comes back', I said, thinking about cats or carrier pigeons. 'No, they don't come back. You have to go out and catch the bugger. They don't go far. But it'll never come back on its own accord.'

P.S. A few weeks after my visit the parrot did in fact fly off again and Biggs never found it. He was very upset and believes 'some thieving bastard stole him'.

Sex in Copacabana
25 July

A few nights after a nice dinner with Biggs and a good chat I wandered into one of those 'sex cabarets' that I had seen dotted around the Copa. In fact it was Biggs who focused my mind that way when we briefly chatted about them. I'd never have ventured in otherwise since they seemed the usual tatty, tired and slightly dangerous places I had seen all the world over. But I was wrong. This wasn't your average 'British' vice with its built-in con and filthy Soho hovel. Nothing is worse, colder, or more depraved than the taste of your *vice anglaise*; its tattiness and shabby, *News of the World*-type thrills. Perhaps a vice reflects the spirit of the country in its true colours. In its entrails so to speak. In Britain vice seeks to cheat you by offering you the possibilities of an excitement it will never fulfil. It regards vice as something extraordinarily nasty that must be savoured in the nastiest way possible – by cheating, stealing the poor tourist's money and flogging cheap wine for fortunes; by making vice something inordinately horrid. The shadow-life of England – its horrible hovels and perverted sex celebrated in such tacky movies as *Personal Services*. Not so here. You are not conned. You pays your money and you see healthy bodies, or healthy-looking bodies, making love . . . or making sex.

So I entered the doors to this club and mounted the stairs to a smallish room with a centre stage thrust out into the centre. On its three sides sat customers, drinking and vaguely watching the show. I was taken in by a waiter and, since I seemed like a tourist, found myself being escorted right to the front in view of the whole audience and the girls on stage.

43

I ordered my compulsory and paid-for beer, and prepared to watch the show.

Six women of moderate attractiveness – which was not a lot – were embracing each other and performing various feats involving much writhing, kissing, and simulated cunnilingus. I had moved swiftly to my table, not wishing to make any dent in the concentration of male faces, but as it was they all seemed to look at the new arrival as if I was an accomplice in the 'crime' and wanted to make sure that I knew that they knew. So I sat, not paying much attention to the labyrinthine mass of entertwined bodies until I had ordered my drink and the waiter vanished. When I looked up and my eyes became accustomed to the gloom it was with a shock that I realised I was given a privileged position as a 'moneyed' type of tourist, and that from the front I looked part of the show. The lights spilled over and on to my table. I watched for a few seconds as hands, mouths and legs were congealing into one huge octopus of flesh, and then I decided to move to the back.

The girls were replaced by two couples – male/female this time – who proceeded to perform in public, conjugal acts. I had never before seen this, but having heard of such things imagined that the acts were simulated, much as actors these days are forced to do in 'serious' movies. I was prepared for the kind of worn-out sex that one might see on the British sex scene. However here it is quite a different kettle of flesh. For one thing, the price of four dollars to include one drink is not going to deplete the tourist's pocket or make him feel ripped off. It's a show like any other and you'd pay the same to see a Samba show or even a great deal more. So the fact that it is a sex show doesn't here automatically mean you pay through the nose and feel privileged to see a peep of nipple. Here it is merely a different type of entertainment. Flesh instead of fowl.

The two couples are reasonably attractive and surprisingly healthy looking with good bodies. The two men look quite athletic and might be going out for a gym display. The music is thumping, the lights are changing and the two couples move together in perfect synchronicity, just bobbing and weaving, and eventually the men have the ladies' knickers off. The customers are fascinated and watch what surely is the most healthy, nourishing and life-giving act nature has ever devised. The fact that it is public is its lurid fascination, even if they could see monkeys doing this every day in Regent's Park Zoo.

The watching faces are now becoming vocal in their appreciation and making encouraging noises to the two pairs who seem quite impervious to it. The two men now have erections of considerable merit on a scale of one to ten they would come close to top marks. Both couples were sleekly built and graceful together, as if they were used to each other and had built up an easy routine. The men now, at the same time like mirror images of each other, penetrated the girls, and in time to the music. They resembled a strange, ritualistic dance. It wasn't even very erotic. It was more clinical and remote and, in its austere performance, strangely beautiful. One woman climbed off her man. He was kneeling back on his haunches demonstrating no wilting whatsoever in his slim, pencil-hard dick that arched upwards. Like a mini-athletic team the two couples prepared again from a different position. What was most impressive was the way the first man made himself totally remote from the audience and performed as if they weren't there. His erection was real and non-passionate and the kind of erection that most blokes get without thinking; a kind of unconscious rising when staring out of a window in a bus and relaxing since there is nothing else to do. Such indolent moments can provoke hards-on. Hards-on are not always the signal for rape-inducing passion. It's almost a reflex action. I think most blokes get H/Os a couple of dozen times a day without thinking too much about it. However this man and his friend were supporting giant ones in full view of a drunken, leering audience, with full lights on and the waiter moving to and fro taking orders for drinks. And yet the performers seemed relaxed in their minds and bodies and were just getting on with the job.

The first couple were investing the coupling with choreo-

graphic variety while the couple behind them performed
theirs with no less diligence and application in synch! I was
more fascinated by the first man since he was nearest to me
and was more of the 'star' of the two couples. His face wore
a totally impassive look and could have been playing Hamlet,
while his mate seemed more vulnerable to the audience's
jibes and had an expression more amused, as if sharing the
joke with them. He also had a very sinewy body but his
moustache gave him the feeling of being half dressed. The
couples appeared to be quite gentle with each other, not to
spoil the equilibrium, especially for the male without whose
appendage the act would not be working.

The whole event took on a less and less erotic flavour and
appeared in a curious way quite ordinary, even admirable.
They were an expert team, as their ease with each other
revealed more and more, and not only practised but in some
way most tender with each other as if they alone knew that
somehow they were made to vilify themselves but were con-
cealing any such feelings from the audience. They had made
a wall between us and them and the music continued to
provide a kind of blanket for them. The music became a
complicit partner and was as guilty, if any were to be guilty
of anything.

A 'horn' is a most temperamental beast that usually will
brook no upstaging by other thoughts. It is likely to leave the
stage if threatened by an unwelcome rival and not return
until that rival has left. So I admired this man more and
more since nature demands in the male a state of mind for
its passions and here was a man who was able to control
them and summon them up with the aid of an attractive
woman in the most hostile circumstances. Here, in spite of
the customers baying and waiters talking he was nevertheless
an ardent lover. I began to admire his courage and heart to
do it, even if habit had 'hardened' him to his task. I admired
them for enduring what most of the world would regard as
degrading and humiliating. But they lost no dignity. We, the
audience, were the animals, leering, jeering, drunk, fat,
greasy and stupid for a night out of raunchy voyeurism. The

performers on the stage were strong and fit and untouched. Here were two couples exposing to the world with ease and dexterity the aesthetics of fucking. Naturally, without perversion or props, just the health and vigour of their own bodies. Society has clothed the sex act with such awesome mystery and power, invested millions in preserving its myth that it is able to reap millions in profits by titillation and indecent exposure; by hinting, playing with, simulating, glimpses of pubic hair, sexist mags – how daring etc., etc. And movies do not hesitate to push willing and unwilling actors into the buff for a touch of fake box office passion. Except that the movie actors fake it for a lot of money and in Rio they do it for real and for a pittance. Is there a difference? I am not sure that the performers in Rio are not more honest. They are poor and poverty has driven them into this situation. Apart from hard-core porn movies the actors in your serious quality movies are not poor, but oblige the stomachs of film producers.

In fact what the two couples did was less harmful to themselves than yobs getting drunk and vomiting all over Leicester Square. The iniquity of massive unemployment plus a callously indifferent regime has created a market in human flesh for the rich tourist who wants to see what Rio is famous for apart from the Samba. However evil the circumstances that created this situation where people could exploit the young bodies of men and women, there was nothing that these people did which humiliated themselves. Rather they stripped away the total hypocrisy surrounding the act and made it as natural and wholesome as playing tennis. It was their achievement that was awesome. That the audience had paid to see images of their own dirty minds exposed had no relation to these four people. Ultimately I felt that the actors and theatre on British stages, with their thin, fakey emotions and watery, expensive productions, were more degrading and far less honest than what I was witnessing here. All that drippy West End howling and screeching about F.A. – how vacuous they seem before the real event of these four young men and women who stripped themselves bare! The real sin is poverty.

They finished their act and left the stage. I felt like cheering their performance. After, in the Boulevard Copacabana, I saw the first couple on their way home. They looked like two serious actors after a heavy workout. Their faces were clean and I could not identify them as anything less than great performers.

Women of Rio
27 July

A major occupation among Brazilian women is trying to pull that tiny lettuce-leaf of cloth out of their asses. You see it on the beach and walking along the promenade, little fingers trying to rescue an inflexible piece of material from obeying the laws of motion. As with the mini-skirt, women are constantly and desperately trying to shorten the distance the eye has to travel to what they feel is the fount of their mystery. Women in minis spend fruitless and trying battles of concealment as they sit, stand, cross their legs, revealing in the transition between positions an 'accidental' exposure of vast expanses of leg. A whole choreographic display is demonstrated as women struggle with their strip of skirt as if they were in battle with themselves, in conflict between exposure and concealment, between liberation and prudery; and so the skirt enabled them to continue their battle almost unconsciously and hypocritically.

They remind me of children who eat around the cherry on the cake, saving the coup for the last. Women have happily nibbled around their private parts for years, attempting to reshape and streamline the body until the focus is purely sexual. The costumes on the beach are cut in one piece that sweeps down to the crutch from high on the hips like a spearhead; or they disappear up their asses in a thong leaving two very often great bulbous cheeks hanging out. The impression is one of total nudity. Perhaps it suggests unconsciously sexual signals to be taken in as an invitation, much like the baboons, who through evolution developed vast, brightly-coloured asses.

The thong is no wider than a piece of dental floss and is

meant to adhere to the crutch, but the more modest tiny handkerchief is one step away and enables the less bold ones to perform the same game as women did with the mini skirt. But having so little to grip, it quickly slides over the precipice and buries itself. And the sight of those endless pairs of fingers, like busy little worms, stretching out the itsy piece of cloth is another one of those eye-catching pastimes for the tourist in Rio. The trouble is that few have the kind of asses you wish to have thrust into your line of vision and you are more apt to gaze disconsolately at four great hanging balloons wobbling like uncontrolled mounds of jelly, pitted like the surface of the moon and lined with cellulite like the canals on Mars. Four, because the girls seldom walk alone. Also the thong costume has other associations that stick like barbs into a overfertile mind.

Men, by contrast, appear at first prudish and sensible in their little boxer shorts. They respect themselves too much to make arses of themselves, and yet at the same time look manly, sexy and good to look at. I suppose women have born the brunt of exploitation for so long that they now allow themselves to be led like cattle to the slaughter, and sacrifice themselves willingly on the altar of fad. To speak true, most look like poor, dumb cattle while the guys look racy, fit, active and uncompromised. Liberation here is a naked bum!

Ronnie Biggs's Party
27 July

Went to Biggs's party yesterday. Rare assortment of people there. The British abroad are a rum lot; not to be compared to those at home. Biggs gets several kilos of meat, chicken and sausages and from time to time, while entertaining his guests, manages to drag out of the fridge huge carcasses of flesh. The scale of everything here is enormous. The smoke rises over the patio and smells good. I arrive just as others are turning up at 1 p.m. It's a whole-day affair and the sun is now blistering down and our small group that arrived dutifully on time huddle in a corner for some shade. Biggs says, 'Help yourself, I'm just going to wash and dig my grave' [shave], and vanishes from our group, leaving us to continue as best we can.

Biggs is like a battery that seems to ignite everyone, and now he's unplugged himself. A huge Londoner with masses of curls decides to occupy centre stage, looking like a right hard bastard. He gleefully demonstrates his broken fist which he complains was badly set by the Brazilian doctors. 'Thumped this geezer on the back of his head. Well, he was reaching for a knife like, and I whacked him ... I did these whorehouse parties in Wapping before they done 'em up ... yeah, thousands turned up.' He's got a house and a pool in Rio. 'Mum says on the phone, "Who does your laundry son?" ... "I got a maid" ... "A maid!" she shrieks ... "Yeah, and a geezer who looks after the pool" ... "A pool!" ' He was evidently chuffed with the contrast of his life in Rio. 'Cor the birds!! ... Do you know they outnumber men by six to one?' I wish I had known that little fact. It might have made me bolder in the knowledge of my own

51

scarcity value. Sod it. I wish I *had* chatted to that blonde on
the beach instead of staring at her rather sheepishly. Six to
one . . . Hmmmmmmn . . . Better get busy.

Two chaps, one British, one American, shooting Martini
ads all over the world, are on the Brazilian leg of the tour.
Red faced, tall Englishman, sweating heavily, upturned nose
you could open a beer bottle with: 'Found these crackers
at the Sheridan but couldn't take them upstairs. It wasn't
allowed . . . Waited till 2 a.m.' British pilot slowly getting
pissed: 'Yeah, I took one up and an hour later two heavies
came to the door and I thought "'Ullo what's this? . . . Are
they looking for bother?" . . . "O.K." I said . . . I started to
shape up' [most unlikely] 'and it turned out they were hotel
security wanting her to check in . . . Yeah, well there was a
spate of robberies and murders so they're checking everyone
now.'

The sun's really beating down now and the dogs are running in and out of the house, and odd people are still turning
up. American boat builder who lives here. Looks fit; silver
haired moustache; looking like we all want to be, secure,
strong, healthy; works with his hands. Even his shorts fit him
well unlike all our baggy ones since we're not yet acclimatised
to what suits us. 'So much violence here I'm moving South',
he said. I was most impressed by anyone who could actually
come to this country from a vastly richer country, not speak
the language and make a good living here . . . and actually
decide to choose between one part of the country and
another. 'I saw three deaths in one day recently', he added.
'I left the house . . . there's a guy lying on the pavement.
Four hours later he's still there in the same position.' What
he said didn't surprise me. There's a lot of wretched people
lying on the streets and when they're sleeping they look a lot
like they could be dead. I mean nobody's going to wake them
up for those domestic demarcations of time that so affect us.
Like 'Wake up, here is your tea', or 'Get up, I want to make
the bed' when you lay on a piece of cardboard. 'Not so much
money in boats in Rio . . . Hard to get spare parts' [Broken
Fist] . . . 'You have to grease the Customs. I got a work

permit but they said at first you have to go to Paraguay, and
then one bloke at the airport said "Give me a hundred and
fifty dollars and I'll stamp your passport" . . . Fantastic! . . .
Now I charge my mates $200!'

I thought about the trip I was forced to do by the film
company. Getting up at 4 a.m. to get the only plane to
Paraguay.

Biggs returned after 'digging his grave', looking well pol-
ished. 'Loads of beer in the fridge. Food coming up in about
an hour.' I sip my *cachassis*. Lovely. Biggs makes a good one;
lots of alcohol and crushed limes. The American touring the
world with the Martini ads is actually making a documentary
about making the commercials. Not much meat in that, I
would have thought. 'There's so much violence in L.A.' he
says. 'Last week someone was shot on the freeway. An angry
driver killed a guy who gave him the finger sign, so now I
carry a 45 Colt in a shoulder holster.' Wearing dark glasses,
portly, silver hair and moustache and knocking back the
booze: 'Loved your work in *Beverly Hills Cop*.' Here we go
again; the film that will haunt me the rest of my life . . .
'Thought number two was crap.' 'Yes' . . . I vainly summon
some enthusiasm for the subject which is about as interesting
to me now as a cup of cold sick . . . 'The first was unique
since Murphy took over from Stallone, so there was an
improvisational feel to it . . . hadn't become a stereotyped
formula . . . Blah blah . . .' 'Oh, Oh', he exclaimed, 'Hadn't
known that.' That's always good for a spittle of reaction.
'Yeah', I gloated, warming to the interest of the boat-builder,
the villain, the 45 Colt. 'Stallone walked off and did *Rambo
2*; pulled me into that having interviewed me and cast me in
the *Beverly Hills Cop*. So two world box office records!!'

The attention was beginning to wander as the sun was
pouring down like liquid butter and was melting my two
world records. The barbecued meat was beginning to insinu-
ate its plumes of smoke into our nostrils and rumbling stomachs. It smelled good and we were wondering when the master
was going to slice it. Dark Glasses returns to his favourite
subject: 'Damn it, I was pulling up in Beverly Hills of all

places. Where I have a house . . . well the whole top floor
of a house . . . when I saw in my mirror this guy walking
slowly to the car . . . As he gets to my window I pulled my
silver Colt 45 and said "Drop it" . . . You should have seen
his face.' Boat Builder: 'Did he have a gun?' 'Sure he did,
in a brown paper bag like they use to carry beer or toothpaste.
"Drop it and walk five paces" . . . I should have blown his
fucking head off.' Suddenly Dark Glasses could have been
cast in Oliver Stone's *Salvador* playing a C.I.A. agent . . .
'Blown the mother fucker away, but who wants to go down
to the cop house so I let the bastard go . . . '

The sun's now starting to ease towards the horizon and I
change the position since I seem to be wedged between Boat-
Builder and Dark Glasses. An attractive couple turn up for
whom the party is in aid: Chris and his wife who could
double for Annie Lennox. 'You look like Annie Lennox', I
dribble. 'Oh thank you,' she beams. She and her husband
sailed from England to Rio in a small boat, stopping off for
a year in Gomera in the Canaries, and had two children on
the way. Then they opened a popular bar here in Rio. 'We
get a lot of gay people in our bar . . . the Brazilian women
are awfully straight.' I thought they didn't look that way to
me. In fact they were particularly curved. 'You're bigger
than I thought you'd be', she observed, staring at my newly
acquired Falstaffian girth, brought about by an overdose of
extreme boredom and *caiperinhas*. Immediately, and in front
of the party which now was getting pretty blowsy since Ronnie's famous meat had not yet been distributed, she pulled
her shorts down, stood there in mini black panties, and
revealed a rather flat plane of stomach, 'Suction', she said
proudly. 'I had a stomach for years, dieted like crazy but
localised fat is the most difficult to get rid of. Had a bit of
bruising but it's worth it.' We all looked at this flat terrain
rather impressed.

Her husband Chris looked like those intrepid adventurers
who are peculiarly English. Thin, gaunt, and traces of an
accent betraying an education that was paid for and dis-
banded. When he talks his eyes seem distantly focused on

far horizons, as if he expected something to rise over the distant smog belt downtown. He was very fond of a certain Brazilian gesture of passing your hand across your face and blowing a kiss as it returns back . . . real approval and so very un-English. Biggsie I notice is also very fond of this Rioccan 'street gesture'. Biggs also has a favourite which is to flick his hand sharply down and thus manage to strike two fingers together to make a snap when he is happy with what you've just said, especially if it carries for him some significance but it can also be used if the food was just that touch special. It's an almost impossible to make and reveals true Brazilian contamination.

The two special guests are sailing back to England and this is farewell bash, although Ron will seize almost any excuse for one. Chris tells me that for them earning money is only the means of tasting new experiences and adventures and not an end in itself. So although his club was doing O.K. in Rio it was now time to pull anchor and leave. The meat was now being carved and a line of hungry, happy people were holding their plates out in the expectation of plenty!' The wait made the food delicious. Some who had already scoffed theirs down held a little shyly back with their empty plates not wishing to appear eager. Ron kept carving and throwing on more sausages and chicken. 'If you don't ask you don't get 'cause if you don't ask you don't want.' This sound piece of philosophy expounded by the carver triggered the right response. The crowd eagerly beavered in, absolved of their guilt.

The sausage was great and the meat cooked to a turn. I started to feel very good here. After weeks of dealing with the film and its tribulations I actually felt restored. The sun set, the parrot squeaked, the dogs yelped and the beer flowed. I saw how in one sense Biggs could be looked upon as a kind of father figure for all the remnants of Britain; a kind of silver haired patriarch lording it over Rio from his eyrie in Santa Teresa. You could always depend on a cold beer and a good chat whenever you saw him. In the far distance one could see the old square rigger sailing ships that had set out nine months earlier to reproduce the historic journey of discovery centuries before. They had moored in Rio having come from Australia to England, and in fact some of the crew were naturally coming to the party and to meet Biggs. Biggs's son Michael is a cheeky bugger who has even recorded his own hit single. He's just turned twelve and greets friends of Biggs with East End familiarities like, 'Hello, you old wanker'. Much like Biggs' parrot he has learned the sacred words straight from the mouth of the master. It was a good party.

Pragmatism; or Trailers
29 July 1987

This film is becoming a humiliating experience, and while most actors don't seem to mind being toe rags and have no interest either way, for me it is a sad misuse of my abilities. The film strikes me as a writer as a putrid and banal exploitation of the facts. And the direction for me is non-existent. We are still battling over what accent to use. It is dangerous to do anything one doesn't believe in, even if it seems fun at first. Last night was a bad evening, and most of the time we were hanging around. When we *were* called it was to walk up and down the stairs fifty times while Paul Freeman as Biggs carried his T-shirts under his arm. On the fiftieth time I moaned aloud to P. F., as is my wont, since this torture is only in relation to what one has done before and if this is what you are used to, then it is just a bore and nothing else. For me it has become a further descent into the swamp. My ego weeps for its humiliation. Up the stair and down the stairs. So I moaned aloud to P. F., who seemed to be taking all this quite normally. I said to him, 'It's gone 6 a.m.' And he, maybe fed up with my moaning, said 'Tell him, not me.'

I was so affronted by his lack of sympathy that I transferred my rage to Lech and said, 'It's 6 a.m. When are we going to finish?' And he replied, 'When we get the shot' . . . and this developed stage by stage, to me calling him a masturbator, since that is all we seemed to be doing all night, and him cursing me in the only way he knows since he is unable to deal with an actor's problem except by confrontation. However, I still believe that human material, while not being indulged, should be respected, and to expect actors to walk up and down stairs for hours is chipping away at the actor's real skills – which is already a hazard of the dreaded film-making and which he expects, but there has to be a limit. You didn't train and study at a drama school and sweat over a line in *Hamlet* to find yourself, at 6 a.m., walking up and down stairs like a zombie, even if you know that film does make the oddest and stupidest demands and you are most willing to whore yourself out to the scummy industry. But even a whore will have her limits.

In the end I had to explain to my colleagues that I was in fact using them as an ear to absorb the overflow of my frustration so that I could be prevented from letting it out on the director. We all use each other to whisper the rebellious things we feel, not always out of cowardice, but we want to avoid the ugliness of confrontation and its effect on everyone. If there is a shoulder nearby, we may lean on it until we have recovered our equilibrium. So my whine was deflected to a 'Tell him, mate, not me' and in my rage I blew a fuse and walked off the set – which is the only time I have done this in my life.

I watched from the bus and changed as they continued to walk up and down the stairs without me, and adjusting the lens not to show a space where once I too strode merrily down. We had spent all night shooting one minute. P. F. did make a rebellion about the trailers – or lack of them – and did a number, even threatening to do a walk-out. In a way he was right since the trailer is a small sanctuary where you can crawl back to a little womb and sleep, fart, write or smoke – whereas tonight we all share a large bus and everyone walks in and out as we try to snatch a few moments of sleep.

I said to P. F., 'Why didn't you support me when I was having a go at Lech on the dreadful conditions we were having to put up with?' He replied that I too hadn't really supported him on the demands for trailers, and he was right. The lack of trailer hadn't bothered me nearly as much as the lack of life and spirit. However, he wisely knew that not much could be done to put life and spirit into the film, but certainly something could be done about trailers, and that is what you call pragmatic. Why torment yourself daily when you can just put your head down and take a deep breath? I started to really appreciate my trailer after this and was most grateful to P. F.

Drift

30 July

Wandered around downtown Rio and slipped lazily in to see *Pirates*, Polanski's latest effort, which, after a brilliant start, seemed to fall apart. Spent the day strolling around favellas and drinking beer in cold, damp, seedy bars, and trying to imagine this is all fun. If the sun ever came out it would all be different, but it seems to have deserted Rio for good. Played billiards with Helmut, my driver, and was astounded at how much it cost to play. Somebody must have money. In the square below from where we were playing I could see forlorn hookers standing around or leaning against the statues. They looked tired and very bored with their life. I'm thinking about *Pirates*, and that keeps me going on this. It looks like Polanski has somewhat lost his bearings, and I imagine that a good dose of me and Kafka will set him back on the track.* I sometimes wonder if, at fifty, you are finished – in the sense of not creating any more masterpieces, just nice bits and pieces that people respect all the more and herald, while having damned your previous vital work.

Escaping to bed early as a release from pain, although the morning was blissful, with a fresh clean look to the sky. Read Desmond Morris's book *The Human Zoo* again and am astounded how twenty years later it all rings so true. 'There will appear', he says, 'a wild fire disease of plague intensity' – and it makes my play *Greek* look more opportune than ever. I didn't know about Aids when I wrote *Greek* in '79. But. . . .

*I am directing Polanski in my version of Kafka's *Metamorphosis*

Grumary Beach

Helmut takes me to a beach about twenty or so miles south, and it's absolutely beautiful – a curved beach with an arm cradling the sea on one side and, at the end, the rock slides into the sea like a giant ski-slope. The waves are larger here and there are few people, and yet you are still serviced by a couple of small shanty cafés on the beach and a giant one just off it, where you can sit, drink and devour your fish accompanied by thousands of flies and hungry dogs. Still . . . take it or leave it, it's still very beautiful. Maybe I'll have a quiet fiftieth here on the beach. That's not bad.

Should love to board a plane tomorrow. Keep dreaming they'll pull the plug on this crap and I can escape. Three weeks and done F.A. If I left, what would be the repercussions?
1. Film would halt.
2. Legal possibilities.
Is there some way out?

Party?

Dreamt I was eating something that had some kind of ant in it, and I complained that I couldn't cut through it, so had to remove the stick-like feelers. It didn't seem unnatural at the time; just repellent. Keeping praying that the film will collapse. Keep asking our line producer, 'Any news?', since the backers are already worried that the film is over schedule and we've hardly started, and I expect Mark Slater's slim figure to come striding along the Copacabana pool, saying 'Take it easy, it's a wrap'. But so far it's only a dream. Still, it's a great morning and sod the birthday party. You don't need it. That's been digging away at my head lately. Mark even kindly offered to organise it for me which takes a burden off my mind. But then I say to myself, do I really want it? I throw up images of a group of people having a good time and it all feels that it is exactly what everybody needs now and would be good for morale. I can even have it at Dietrich's house on the hill that his brother Helmut organised; and it's a stunning house, set in its own grounds, overlooking Rio; and we could make barbecues. And so the party is beginning to look good again.

Night
31 July
Smoke

Night work. I hate it. Called at 8.30 p.m. and still hanging around 2½ hours later. It's 10.45 p.m. Angst about party which, for a few hours of dubious pleasure, is hardly worth the sweat thinking about it. Who will come? Will they all come? . . . etc. Ron Biggs suggests we do a double since his birthday is one week later. So that's fortuitous, and doesn't make mine such an event like 'It's my birthday number. How sweet.' So if Biggs joins in I can almost sit on the sideline. We'll split costs and people. But suppose he brings his whole clan? Then it becomes his birthday which I am half paying for. Then I start to worry again and realise that it all doesn't matter and that I am letting the event of the 'FIVE O' get to my craw. In fact it would be good for Biggs and his mates to come, and whoever else.

The film is beginning to drive me crazy. The atmosphere on the film is crappy and it hardly calls for a party, although everyone here would like it. Everybody seems to be turned into a group of clinker collectors – including me. I'm beginning to feel like a toe-rag employee, eager to pick up little sphincters of news regarding Lech. Wondering what the future holds. Will we continue? Will we go on location to Paroti* or not. Whispers go around the troops and I dutifully pass mine on. I search faces for missing clues. Will Mark's twisted smile mean that the film is going down the drain, or has he got constipation from too much meat? Jessel, the first assistant, knows nothing yet, but he has the ear of the producers. I constantly search his face and question him.

*Paroti is a beautiful and colonial town 250 miles south and totally preserved in its 18c setting. Was the original administrative capital.

'What's happening Jessel?'

'I don't know my friend.'

'Do you think we'll wrap?'

'If I knew I would tell you.'

'I think all this is insane.'

'I agree with you. It's absolutely crazy.'

At least we're in trailers – thanks to the explosion of P. F. I sit back and wait. There's nothing in the small fridge each trailer has. Must remind myself to get some beers. And so my mind drifts in and out of focus, hearing the noises just inches from my small thin walls. Let the party go on. Really don't want this party! What dreams I had of celebrating my fiftieth in Rio, and what a dreary bore it has turned out to be.

George, the cinematographer, says that people laugh at stuff in the rushes. I suddenly feel encouraged, but I also have the feeling that it will end up on the cutting room floor. It's 2.35 a.m. I was here at 8.30 p.m. and have hung around for six hours and done nothing but eat, sleep and drink coffee. [But I'm getting used to the slow pace.]

This is the slowest film in history. The long hours just drift away in the warm square. We did one page. A whole night's work. One page a day equals three months at least. Maybe Lech is a perfectionist and what we see will justify this. And there is certainly no doubt that he takes his work very seriously. But, *one page!*

Decided against party. Just have an evening with Clara when she arrives. Best. Don't and yet do want it. Something to remember my birthday in the end. A few drinks will be enough . . . downstairs maybe, in the hotel. Dinner for all at some fancy place maybe? But don't let it bother you. Don't half think through something and then sweat on it for five days. Do it!

The square is lit by rain and gleams under the arc-lights. It hasn't rained, but a truck was hired to spread it round the square. Who thinks of these things? All these details, like a shiny wet street? And so the van sprays the square and by the time we shoot the square is dry again. Is it my imagination and the square was merely and routinely sprayed by the street cleaners? But I don't think so. We sit and eat and take up my time and chew on the chicken and absorb the smells of the trees and the fresh air since we're high up.

Eventually we start and all pile in the Mercedes belonging to one of the backers who doubles as an assistant. Roberto gets the car going but it keep stalling, and so we have to be rescued – revved up – and we go again. Peter Firth drives. We hit the marks and see a fire in the street – which is supposed to be my intro to Macumba*. The car stops and I look out and see the smoke and the bottle of booze left for the spirits. Lech shrieks 'More smoke!' to the man up the street. A second prop man is further up the street and he thinks the call is for him and starts the smoke canister. Then various people run up the road to correct the excess or lack of smoke. 'MORE SMOKE!!!' . . . 'ACTION' . . . 'Too much smoke!!' . . . 'CUT' . . . 'Much less smoke this time' . . . 'ACTION!' . . . more smoke . . . less smoke . . . more smoke . . . less smoke . . . Cut. Action, Cut, Action, Cut . . . Far too much smoke! Too much fucking smoke!! Action . . . More . . . That's O.K. . . . We got it . . . Action . . . More smoke. Cut! Tell him, Julia, to give less smoke. Action Cut. Action Cut. Action Cut. Goodnight!

3,000 people?
Friday 31 July

Fri. After a splatter of rain this morning it settled down. Ate breakfast on the balcony. My usual papaya, melon, croissants and coffee. And write. Facing the flakey grey-green sea. I like to get up as early as possible, when they start serving breakfast at 6 a.m., so I can see the night streaking away. Had weird dreams. Was in N.Y. with Shelley, my ex-wife, sitting in a café where two girls were rudely staring, as they do (movie fame!). We moved, and I looked out of the small

---

*Macumba is the semi official voodoo rites. Combining occult of region plus S. American Indian with even bits of Christianity thrown in. A belief in spirits both good and evil.

window. It was like somebody's front room; but high up. As I leaned on the window to get up it just fell away. I could have been killed. I complained but nobody took any notice since they were too concerned about the window rather than my close brush with death. We left; walked down the stairs, and each step had somebody's sweater or books on it and, again, one could have tripped, and so I picked my way carefully down. Somebody said, 'Sorry, but it's only a student's "forcing house" where they cram for exams.' The window was interesting . . . What does that mean? Whatever I touch crumbles? Now, as I type this journal, I sense what it means. Does it say that the film I am in is like this house – precarious and full of hidden obstacles that the carelessness of students or beginners has put in my way? Not malicious, but simply inexperienced. Very Kafka. His works were written with the intense logic of dreams.

Last night L. called for a pointless rehearsal at the hall where 3,000 people are rumoured to be crammed. Most unlikely, but the talk had been going round for days with the magic figure 3,000. Everybody was getting excited about it, like this was real big movies. 3,000 extras – the word spun round the make-up dept, the actors, the wives of the demi-producers. I knew about it, and the figure was shot into my ears as if this would finally assure all of us that we are making *movies!* It was going to be an event at any rate. A packed hall, jammed tight with 3,000! Sweating, moving bodies, undulating to the fierce percussions of the *batteria*. The cast and technicians (which meant, and usually meant, make-up, hair, wardrobe and crowd control – in the shape of a yuppish American assistant) would jig their hips all night long as they went about their business; and when people spoke to you they would do so while waving their hips from side to side, as if this had nothing to do with them but was an involuntary spasm.

In the event, I think, we would be lucky to see 1,000 – which would be a sizeable sum. But the estimate that the entire club membership of 3,000 would turn up, just for some free beer and a possibility to be in a film, was a wild overestimate. There would be some 'wowy' shots, and some creative dicks would be jerked. Good luck to them; and this is what film is for. 'Sound' again will have no meaning whatsoever and will be dubbed in the cold studios of Pinewood in future times.

So we walked through the hall making mental notes about where we would be; but how we would shoot in the noise I do not know. Lech was valiantly trying to summon up my enthusiasm as he explained everything to me, but I just nodded, resigned to it all, and already too demoralised by the prior events to expect anything less than torture.

Without my being an Elijah, my prophecies were right. However, I warm to his enthusiasm and pigheadedness. I'm sure he doesn't *mean* to torture us. Or does he? He flogs on, followed by his long shadow, Julia, who, like an adoring belt, holds the whole edifice together.

Bought a chess set and enjoyed using my brain for the first time in ages. Played P. Freeman and we won and lost by turns. It was almost enthralling. Then I played a curious Jewish Argentinian who may put some money in the film and dealt in war supplies in the shape of bullet-proof jackets. He complained about the food on the set, which I thought was rather good. On Monday I would have been here four weeks. Amazing. Four weeks of mind bending torture. For me anyway. But something like a book will come of it!!! Something will always come of something.

The party biz is getting me down. Don't want to do it. It has to be on the day! Mark was positive and reassured me that he would take care of all the logistics, like getting people to the location and supplying vans to the house; and Ida, his lady, would arrange the catering with Biggs if we do a joint effort. Use the opportunity. You're not working since it's Monday. The house is there. A group of people hungry for it.

Desmond Morris never ceases to fascinate me. He writes, that we keep infantile behaviour patterns by staying home way past the time we should, due to economic dependence. We are living in the parent-child hegemony way past the time it should have shrivelled away, and the parent rarely changes his or her attitude, and so the young adult is kept in a state of arrested development for years after. At fifteen we are physically and morally brave and adventurous enough to produce good offspring, and have great stamina. But we are kept at home into our twenties and beyond. We emerge from the home as mother-fucking assholes and turn our wives into surrogate mothers. The women are not much better; particularly American women with a strong tendency to whinge and tell tales after school.

He who needs must Kowtow
or
The Armpit of the Snake

The thing is not to need, and you are never disappointed. You flow into the inner river of yourself which supplies all the needs you could possibly desire. The greatest entertainment zone; the most magical video system. Look how two men are fascinated by a game of chess; a few pieces to joggle round the board and an hour's rapt concentration. I needed the chess, the computations and forward thinking. In the end I decided to go for the party, even if I think it would have been stronger to ignore such vanities. Since I am in the conditioned mode, let's do it.

After work – and it wasn't too late since we are still in the early stages – we went to a café/bar called 'The Armpit of the Snake'. Good title for a film. P. Free and I, along with the arms dealer, visited this place that Paul had discovered and enthused about. Bit of local colour. So we found it about to close but still going strong while a few clients came by. It had to be about 3 a.m. So we took our seat outside and ordered some drinks. An old fat lady sang into an over-amplified system. Every time she took a breath her stomach shot up a notch and was intensely watchable, although she sang well – like she was an old favourite there. It was a cruddy but sweet little bar, and even in such a hole the waiters served you in white shirts and little black ties. Young people inside the café seemed to enjoy the old and dated Samba tunes, and danced on each other's thighs. This has to be Paris in the forties.

Then a middle-aged man took over the mike. He turned out to be a taxi driver who, when he got bored, swung his cab over to the Armpit of the Snake and entertained the customers for a while. He was a gifted amateur, except that he seemed to be made of concrete from the neck to the waist; but he moved easily from there down. His movements were like everything you ever saw in every pop programme all your life, except moving like he was in a straight jacket. After a while he started to depress me terribly, but he sought everybody's approval after each singing bout, staring hopefully at us all, as if he had acquitted himself beyond his dreams and sought in our faces some confirmation of his neglected skill. After a while the belly came back and sang loudly, loosely, and emotionally; and it was a welcome relief.

Churascurio, or the Meat House

A way of cooking meat on charcoal; barbecued. A meat house like no other. Here in Brazil everyone who can afford it eats meat with a vengeance. It is the staff of life. It represents the wealth of Brazil: the vast ranches and endless tons of meat that go through the stomach. Not for Brazilians the lean or *nouvelle cuisine*, or culinary pampering for neurotic, water-drinking designer vegetarians. Here meat is ubiquitous like the smog: wherever you go you will smell the tang of roasting meat in the air: in the cafés, bars, butchers; on street stalls sold on sticks and dipped in hot sauces, in snack bars, on the beach, in pasta, as an *apperitivo* in a bar where a group of people will share a dish of finely sliced fillet cooked with spring onions and spear it with tooth picks, in pubs sliced in sandwiches, and finally, the king of them all, the *churascurio*.

Here you sit and the waiter brings to your table every kind of meat from all parts of the animal, so you are not restricted to your rump steak and chips. First he comes and dulls the edge of your appetite slightly by offering you a salad plate, which includes the delicious heart of palm, soft and textured like marble. Then along comes the waiter with the meat; like heralds bearing scrolls they enter with these long skewers of meat which have been charcoaled and burnt fiercely on the outside and when sliced reveal the pink flesh beneath. So it has also a slightly erotic undertone, as if the delights were 'revealed' by the slicing off of the overgarment. It's only salted on the outside; no other flavour used in the charcoaling except its own juices.

The waiter carries the skewer of sizzling meat in both hands while bearing in his lower hand at the same time a little silver bowl in which to catch the fat; not always successfully it would seem, since the floor of this particular café is like a skating rink. One waiter may again offer you a starter, like sausages or chicken, and if you demur another waiter is speeding swiftly toward you with the giant stick from which he will slice off a section of the prepared meat and swiftly return the shaved skewers of meat to the burning coals for sealing. You've hardly finished your slice when the waiter glides back with his sizzling rump or sirloin on its iron skewer, holding the other end in its metal cup. With a razor-sharp knife he slices it slowly from the top and it falls gradually away, but before it reaches the end of its journey onto your plate you are invited to spear the meat with your fork to prevent it slapping inelegantly down. A thin slice, darkly barbecued on one side and virgin on the other. Another waiter will come by, offering kidney, liver and other delicacies, but you will safely remain with fillet or rump. It tastes unlike any other meat. It tastes supremely good.

I am plummeted back to my heady old meat-eating days, before conscience, ecology and additives diminished my desire for the red flesh . . . when meat was wholesome to a growing child, like the slice of bread Mum dipped into the stewpot, held it out sopping and tasting more wonderful than anything on earth. In later years, living with and knowing vegetarians has opened all the doors of the most divine world of taste. The meat sitting in the fridge on a white plate onto which blood had oozed out was a thing of the past. That slightly sick feeling when you slice a steak and it's just too raw and you are inevitably reminded that it is blood which is leaking out of that piece of meat, however much it is decorated with sauce and peppercorns and surrounded by innocent little sprigs of parsley, as if to help you reduce the slaughter on your plate. Here meat is and feels like sin, and makes no pretence of avoiding its role with décor. Just plain meat.

The white-jacketed waiter approaches. You have never tasted meat so good, whose only flavouring is salt – they don't even serve mustard. And you don't have to send it back since it comes as raw or as well done as you wish. Biggs introduces me to a good *churascurio* and interprets each offering: 'Try the lamb, this is the shoulder, and what do you think this is? Have a guess?' . . . Could be turkey. He seems to know intimately each part of the animal – the shin, thigh, topside – introducing each one like guests arriving at a party.

Offerings are now coming more quickly, before you've even had time to denude your plate – roast beef, turkey wrapped in bacon. The waiter skews off a couple and you get back into the act, washing it down with a good glass of *caiperena*. A chunk of mignon. The knife flashes and the meat slaps down onto your plate, with you obeying the ritual with your fork, guiding it gently down to land. The slices are not too thick – just sufficient each time to have you wanting more. It's heady stuff. The pork's declined. No more chicken or sausage. This is certainly a place for serious indulgence and it needn't cost a fortune. Sometimes there is in all of us a desperate need to pig out, to indulge in some carnal offering, be it flesh, eaten or desired.

The knife again slashes through, and there is no inclined eyebrow by any waiter since this is what you are here for. The meat sizzles and the fires roar in the distant open kitchen. The smell is good, and now I fee my waist pushing against my belt and relax from the kill and look around at the other carnivores. They don't actually look too healthy, I force myself to admit. A man on the next table is so obsessed with his piece of meat that he is trying to swallow the whole slice and the meat that remains outside his mouth hangs down like some disgusting tongue . . . I turn away promptly from the hideous sight . . . I glance at the other customers and see some solitary eaters like myself, but older, rich looking men with yellow faces for whom company is a piece of dead meat being brought smoking to their plate. I begin to feel as if I am at debauched gathering . . . carnal desire here takes on a new meaning. It's easy to eat since you never see a giant fillet steak on your plate, but only a slice at a time, and when it comes to your plate it almost looks like a piece of burnished wood. It looks too good to refuse.

You forget just how many slices you have had . . . six, eight, ten, twenty? The offering continues to dance in and out of your vision and you begin to decline and slow down and yet meat is the one thing you can still eat after real hunger has long abated. It longs for your bite and the taste clings to your teeth and I suspect you must be fulfilling or awaking atavistic longings . . . you feel bestial as you disturb some primitive appetite. I glance at myself in the mirror on the wall to check myself . . . Do I look evil yet? Gloating? Wolfish? I imagine that I would start to reveal signs of the sweaty, yellow demeanour of the compulsive meat eater. But I am disappointed to see I look more or less the same as when I walked in. Obviously it hadn't taken its toll yet. I pay the bill, which comes to 400 *cuizeros* – which is a blow out for less than four pounds. I have feasted, if not with panthers, at least like a panther. But a small puritanical streak in me makes me feel as if I have been to a brothel. A bit of an orgy, what?

The Others
31 July

Up at 6.30 a.m. and wrote a piece on guilt which I think is
O.K. – so I haven't been wasting my time. Then had a short
run and did a few arm dips on the parallel bars that they
have on the beach here, so you don't have to join a gym –
you just go out to the beach and work out in the open air. I
love things that are free and put there by the municipality –
it takes a pressure off your life and you feel a sense that
somebody does care. Anybody can go and train – like the
paddle tennis courts and handball courts in Venice L.A.
Money is a great divider and beaches and the like are great
mixers and equalisers. It also reminds me of the recreation
parks we used to run into when we were kids that were full
of all kinds of mysterious contraptions. So I did sets of 15
arm dips, but didn't dare risk yet pull-ups at the bar. Swam
in the sea and then in the hotel pool.

Wandered outside to one of the cafés to have a coffee and
write. Poor little black girl sitting all clean and neat and
looking for a client.

Just met Richard Dreyfus, looking very pale and with white
bandy legs, but he was very pleasant and was sitting round
the pool with Paul Mazursky who made some very nice
comments about my play *Greek* which was shown in one of
those 'showcase' theatres in L.A. of all places. Paul M. is
making a film here with a budget of about $16 million and
is in the process of rehearsal and is working with the actors
for two weeks before shooting any film. Raoul Julia is also
sitting there, and Sonya Bragg. So this is the other film which
shall from now on always be a yardstick to compare with our
dawdles as they go confidently from day to day, always on

schedule, using thousands of extras, changing locations overnight and even being a day or two ahead. The actors will meet by the pool or the restaurant, or even in the lift, and say 'How's it going?' And I will shrug and murmur something, not wishing to shed too gloomy a note each time we meet. And I will ask him and the answer will always be couched in enthusiasm.

The difference in the social life of the American and British group is that they are always together, sitting by the pool with their director, as if they genuinely loved being together, while we, in true Brit fashion, go our own ways. However the Brits are always independent, and a star like Richard Dreyfus may have to be cautious in a place like Brazil. Anyway Americans are a more friendly, relaxed type of people, and I feel like joining the 'other' side. Paul even asks me if I want to do a day on his picture, just for the fun of it, and I can't say yes because our schedule is so changeable while theirs is cast iron.

Raoul walks around with a Harrison Ford hat on the whole time and keeps much to himself, while in the next weeks they will be joined by their wives and their nannies. Later Paul F. will have his wife, nanny and kid and all the nannies will sit by the pool and commiserate with each other about the lack of cable T.V. in their rooms. This fact will become so serious that members of the P.M. film will leave the Copacabana Hotel – which is one of the most beautiful hotels on earth – and move into the plastic tower down the road which doesn't even have balconies on which to eat your morning papaya, but what it does have is . . . *cable TV!*

I found over the weeks Paul Mazursky's friendliness quite moving, and never did it vary in the two months we were sharing the hotel, nor did I ever see him in anything less than high spirits, and if he did have problems I have never seen a person cover them up so well. He would always have a story on the tip of his tongue and be the first to leave his table to say hello to you. Altogether he was a formidable bloke.

The Party
1 August

Arranged party after all, and then completely relaxed. Ida's handling it and I just turn up. Terrific. Almost feel proud. Had thought of a dinner somewhere – but where? – and now this gives something to everyone! Bravo! Mix the the two film crews up a bit – Mazursky and his lot, and ours. Now it's raining and that fucks everything up. Not necessarily.

Did my usual walk and photographed a woman holding a baby in one arm and selling chiclets in the other. My midday *caiperena* tastes good. I think when you obey your instincts it all comes out all right. Good old Mark and Ida; and it gives people something to do. I cry at the thought of my half century. Fifty feels pretty good really. I'm fairly fit, a bit overweight, not too many lines; less stressed looking than I used to be; not a bad home; written fifteen plays – some of which may be classics and will be performed when all my contemporaries will be dead in flesh and spirit since their works lack the spirit to make them last.

Picked up a play by a successful English writer much in vogue and couldn't get past the first page. It didn't mean anything to me and lacked an inner sound. It wasn't coming from his guts. You can always tell. He had something he wanted to say, but it was what he believed he should talk about – it was all in his head.

Working tonight with thousands of people. Secretly pleased I bought the small camera. Mustn't be so self-critical.

A cool Saturday. The nightmare continues. Was relieved to cancel my party this week after talking to Biggs who wants to be involved. So we shall make it a double birthday for the following week and it will give us more time for preparations.

Biggs is a great party giver and gets down to the nitty gritty straight away. Ida hadn't done a thing yet. 'I didn't have any money', she wailed. Then she said she rang round a few friends and I got panicked thinking we are going to have everybody and that I am paying for a freebie for all their mates. My paranoia was taking hold of me. Rather less people than more, but I don't want to seem tight-assed. Don't want to enter a house full of strngers. There should be about 70. Mark says sagely that parties need a certain 'density' to take off. He sounded expert suddenly. That's what my parties have always lacked. Density. I kept looking at the door wondering when everyone was going to come and hoping for that frisson. That *density*. But I enjoyed Biggs's party immensely last week since I could talk to everyone there. So you don't need this mass. There was a mass at that fucking awful party the week before and it was noisy and dreadful.

Last night was a sheer nightmare, thinking about the party in my trailer, and the noise in the stadium of the band, and the incessant sameness of the music; and then walking up and down the floor following Paul as he shows me around Rio as Biggs. The shit that actors do. So I had to follow his ass across the floor feeling like a jacketed turd. We are just figures in a stream of images. Ronnie is there and keeps me sane with his humour and his easy attitude. I shouldn't have said to Mark that he shouldn't bring too many friends. Why not. I always put my foot in the shit and slide. A low period in my life. The night shoots are terrible – especially with these lunatics – and the text is thrown out of the window. We just shout and the story goes down the drain. Should never have got on the plane.

Sat. 12 p.m.

But for Biggs I might have caved in. As it is, it's much lighter and almost tolerable. I blew up as the meaninglessness of the exercise made me feel utterly useless and wasted. I feel I have never wasted my life so pointlessly before. And to taste fifty in such a depressing job ... to end on this note.

Something has to come of it. *PLEASE!* Keep debating walkout until conscience is able to defeat pain. Self knowledge, as Jung says, is worth all theoretical knowledge.

3 August 1987; Mon. 3 a.m.

It gets worse and worse. Some kind of horror creeps over me. I have to escape. Grotesque abuse of performers spending all night doing a scene of walking up and down stairs, or spending hours driving pointlessly around. All this will be cut.

4.10 a.m.

Never looked forward to a day off so much. This is it. The big one; and feel nothing. A few faces wish me a happy birthday and it feels really warm. Strange how such a thing as a good wish can still affect you. Never thought I'd see it. It just sneaked in.

5.02 a.m.

It becomes horrible again with the constant 'Do it again'. He's killing all possibility of joy in one's work, or even interest. It's evil to be in such a position of helplessness. Can one just abandon this dreek. Possibly though it's not as horrible as yesterday since there's a bit of acting required today. The poor actress is new to the set and is already suffering this overkill on this slim, petty little script. Logically I suppose one is employed to do this garbage and, as an employee, one has to do it. Now all the players here can't stand the work, with me possibly as chief loather. I should love to go tomorrow. What repercussions? They'd quickly recast. Or disband completely. I can't leave since we hope the worst is over. We are still doing this small scene six hours later. The actress gave her all. Eventually it was cut out of the film!

Action!

'Steven!' A voice seemed to call from down immense corridors, floating and tapping at the room in which I keep my brain. 'Steven' – again – the sound more insistent as the brain floats in its dark tank. A velvet curtain rises as an eye opens itself. 'Steven, you're wanted on the set.' The eye opening rushes the horrible info back to base, to the deep labyrinths where the brain lies cushioned and drugged by sleep, its automatic pumping, breathing and circulatory systems working while the pilot drowses himself in dreams, which are really parables by which the mind solves its problems. The info now received is the interior of a small trailer in a backstreet in Rio. A table with a half finished chess game with Paul Freeman; bits of tangerine peel; a semi-comforting paperback of Jung's *The Inner Self.*

I try to suck from whatever source some comfort against the relentless assault of making this film. I feel I am climbing Everest without a guide or having my brain operated on by a motor mechanic. An endless trial and error; well meant no doubt, and honest in intent, but intentions do not lead to victory. The actors are dragged hither and thither along the quicksands, getting bogged down and then pulled out; shooting scenes for hours that prove to be out of focus and useless since the demands on the very able camera operator were too complicated. Too much movement for the poor man to catch up; a shade out and its ruined; mouthing lines that would not do credit to an orang-utang; plots that are constantly in contradiction to the laws of reason and yet, like the crew on the Bounty, we are led on, less by our convictions – which have long parted from the souls of the actors – than by a sense of guilt. As your spirit rises to revolt and tear yourself away, your guilt crawls out of the debris and whispers in your ear, 'How can you do this to the poor man? Think of all the 'work' already sunk into the enterprise.' Also the weakening and debilitating journey reduces your resistance as each day you think must be your last, and yet another day opens out like a great yawning abyss to swallow you up.

My eyes opened. 'Steve . . . You're wanted on the set.'
The third assistant who called me could have said 'You're
needed on the galley under Captain Bligh.' I crawl out of
the warm tunnels of sleep into the raging blasts of man-made
sickness and despair that surrounds this little trailer in the
back streets of Rio. The stench of urine is beginning to crawl
into my awakening senses. We're shooting outside one of the
giant 'Escola de Samba' halls where thousands of people
come each weekend, listen to songs and dance and fraternise;
where the music shatters your eardrums and you get a little
drunk and have a good time. Outside the hall are little stalls
roasting meat on skewers and other delicacies. But tonight
we are 'recreating' the atmosphere. We've been doing this
for a week and it's beginning to pall as I hear the same songs
pounding out of the dance hall and the high pitched whine
of a mike 'shorting' and the eternal testing . . . 'Allo, allo,
allo, allo . . .' 'SHUT UP!' I scream, to no avail but my
jangled nerves which are momentarily anaesthetised by my
howl.

I put on my ill-fitting grey suit with a cheap silvery sheen
– 'Makes you look like a knight' – and totally out of character
shirt and tie. I loathe the uniform of my slavery, especially
as it's such a disgustingly bad fit. I limp on to the set. The
weight of my heart is like lead and my feet very reluctantly
follow each other, feeling like Clarence – 'Go tread the path
that thou shalt ne'er return'. At dawn we must stop as the
first light creeps through the windows and the editor sweetly
says that we can't shoot any more. But now it is a mere
midnight and as usual some cretin has called me hours early
since they have no conception of the chemistry of actors
who are best at working in short bursts like hundred metre
sprinters. They are not long distance joggers. To call an
actor indifferently early merely to keep him stewed in his
trailer for hours rotting away in spirit is likely to produce in
him unsavoury thoughts and little worms of doubt creep in.
A feeling of worthlessness then becomes pervasive and when
he is eventually called the performance he then gives is
guaranteed to be lack-lustre and forced.

We're on the set. A group of extras are told to dance and they dance on the spot to silent music which looks both funny and macabre. The women try to look sexy in golden leotards and feathers atop high heels. But they tend to appear slightly wasted and sallow although some are quite pretty; yet their skin looks unhealthy and scabby from constant meat eating and little balance in their diet. They dance away, dutifully wobbling their bums. The director instructs a half asleep wooden actor in the dull mechanics of the staging which usually implies filling the camera with as much action as possible while you are acting out a scene. Rails are laid down for the camera to roll on, mounted by our enthusiastic cameraman whose excitement in shooting his first film is matched by an almost innocent childlike joy when he gets it in focus.

My accent as the Scots cop out to get Biggs roams around the Glasgow of my youthful theatrical training and generally ends up as a homage to Sean Connery. We tend to so scenes over and over again which, rather than perfecting a scene, tends to chew it to death. P. Freeman says, parodying Sartre, 'Hell is being here for ever doing the same scene directed by Lech.' We continue the scene until the Brazilian actress who has a high reputation in the film world can no longer make sense of the lines. Extras are shunted across our paths to keep the liveliness going in the dance hall until we are all but buried in extras, and sometimes I become a pair of eyes peering through an undergrowth of arms and heads. The extras near us are all furiously dancing and never seem to hear the word 'Cut' and so continue their silent dance. It resembles a *danse macabre:* 50 poor extras condemned forever to dance since the director forgot to say 'Cut'.

After each 'take' the director comes over to give notes. The actors hear them and, while trying not to look bored, attempt a kind of neutrality upon which the director can read what interpretation he will. We now reverse shots and this will take an hour to reset the lights. An hour of respite. We head back, disconsolate figures, to our little trailers and dreams. We dream of better times. We compare this to other

movies and this comes low on our ratings. We appreciate the
days when filming was at least fun and not torture. The past
rushes at us with comforting memories. We dream of the
end and even secretly pray for some abrupt abortion of the
whole thing. I write; we play chess; fall asleep. Momentarily
the waves close in and once again my brain is cosseted away
in some safe harbour. A brain is an endangered species and
should be protected from assault.

Through the darkness ... 'Steven! ... Steve? ... Your
call.' Like the rushing of waves parting I rise from this half
asleep, the way you wake in prison with the taste of the day's
horror to come. Not at home awakening to a sweet breakfast
or a loved one; waking should be where possible a carefree
experience and not 'Oh my God, where am I?' The stink
outside has wafted in the open door as the messenger gives
you the news that it's your 'close-up'. You feel like death as
you once again clamber into your suit and noose your neck
with a drab tie. The sound man turns you into a radio
receiver. Hands pull you this way and that. A girl slaps some
makeup on your face and again you march those weary steps
to hell. At least the other actors are lines 'off'.

Your C/U. Rehearse and then do it. 'Was my hand in my
pocket?' The extras go into their dance of death. I grab a
whore; she goes to slap me and I seize her hand at the last
split second. It's O.K. and the words are remembered and
the dumb dancers continue long after '*Cuuuuut!*' It's now
5.30 a.m. We have been here since 8.30 p.m. the previous
night. 9½ hours on one small scene of less than two pages;
but there's a lot of crowd and 'action'. '*Actshuuuun!*' he
screams, and again it's O.K. My Scots accent doesn't quite
sound so barky and it nearly feels like regular filming. But
we go again ... and again ... and again ... and.... But
now the editor comes up. 'The light's coming through the
windows and you can't do much more.'

We finish and I salute the dawn. It saved us like a welcoming Greek god dragging the chariot of the sun to bring the
world life, light and nourishment ... plus an end to this.
Hell was being diluted by the fires of Apollo. 'Wrap' ... the

magic word. I tear off my dismal weeds and am myself once more. Oh sweet dawn, I do salute thee with breakfast on my balcony of the Copacabana Hotel and the papaya tastes particularly good and the sea is calm. Another night over . . . Oh thank God. 'Cut!'

2 p.m.

So, after this awful night had breakfast and little sleep and Helmut took us to the beach at Grumari where we had a birthday lunch on the beach. The sun came in and out and it felt good to be there with C. who had just arrived. We found one little snack bar open and drank *caiperenas*, and the woman cooked a huge slab of fish and we ate it with some wonderful chips and it was the most peaceful way I could imagine spending my fiftieth.

Humiliation
5 August 1987

Wed. Last night's work encouraged me to think we could move faster through this garbage, but tonight we are back in turgid hell again. The awful, over-amped music in this giant Samba hall being repeated over and over again. The lousy, gormless scene. Folk in future times reading these words may wonder how I put up with this twaddle for so long. Berkoff, the governor of himself, turns into this heap of pleading shit, wearing these awful clothes, doing these mindless actions; suffering a hell like never before. To be an actor can be hell when doing somebody else's turgid rubbish. Probably, if you have never written yourself, you allocate a part of your being as an appendix for the puerile work you are forced to do and say, but when you have had the freedom of your own expression it becomes monstrously difficult to suspend judgement. The humiliating actions with laughing gas that was once one of the 'highs' requisite for your enjoyment at Carnival time, though seldom it ever used now – not that this makes any difference to our director once he got to hear of it. So in it goes along with everything else.

Oh well, more making an ass of myself. A scene I am dreading. Does one have to do everything you are told? I am hellishly reminded of the helium mask Frank uses in *Blue Velvet* that, amongst the other unconvincing 'tasks', convinced me not to do it – and when I saw it I felt totally vindicated and grateful to Dennis Hopper whose career started to fester again. Just do it and don't give a shit . . . NO DON'T! Hell *is* other people. Sartre is so right. The scene we waited all night to do, that was worth keeping a bunch of valuable actors waiting hours to perform, was rushing out of this dump 'dancing' and led joyfully by a woman who sprayed laughing gas in our faces. The young woman was obviously thrilled to be playing in this 'international' movie and kept warming up in front of us, to all our embarrassment, with some dance disco type movements. She was taking this very seriously, which somehow made it worse, and Paul Freeman is pretending it's not hell and all is O.K. As Biggs, P.F. was asking *me* to 'loosen up' . . . me, the loosest actor on earth, being asked to loosen up. So I fake loosening up and looking awkward, as the character should in fact – an uptight Glaswegian cop. But poor Paul Freeman has no such compensations. He *is* Biggs and therefore must be 'loosened up' . . . After all, he is instructing me to be more like him.

Paul is dressed becomingly in white, like a cricketer, and moving his hips from side to side in what he must hope is a faithful emulation of a Samba, and the long thin tart who is still doing her disco movements is now expressing some kind of hideous 'joy' on the takes. It's now 4 a.m. Not only am I tired out of my mind, I am tired of trying to bolt back my degradation the way a man tries to hold back his vomit. P.F. has just done a scene demonstrating his prowess on a drum called a *cuíka*,* which has a stick in it and when pulled makes a whining sound or a farting sound according to your mood and who plays. I have an immortal line as I pass him . . . 'What's that Biggsie? . . . a wanking machine?' . . . Ay, it's all good stuff.

The orchestra – or *batteria*, as it is called, since it is like being battered by sound – is actually a small, well-drilled unit of percussionists who make the most powerful thunderclap of sound. It's like the sound barrier being broken by a score of jets. It rips through the Samba hall and sends your pulse racing. There is nothing quite like it since it expresses the full power of male energy – fierce, ecstatic and explosive. The female dances to this energy with the full force of her own power, her hips moving like snakes, her spine like a whip-lash. The men, who are mainly mulattos, hit the drum

*Actually a *cuíka* is shaped like a small barrel open at one end. The stick attached to the skin at the other end produces an animal-like ululation.

with a hard thwack from boney, sinewy hands. The leader
stands in this epicentre of energy and controls them to stop
at a split second's notice and to start the same way. It does
not build, but ignites in one terrifying explosion. In the
middle of this raucous Afro/Brazilian cacophany of Latin
power sits P. F., pulling his piece of string in his *cuíka*. He
smiles and nods his head from side to side in obedience to
the rhythm – an actor trying not to look out of place. What
on earth is he doing there? Did the real Biggs occasionally,
and for a laugh, sit in once with a small group of musicians?
Even so, how could it justify P.F. gigging in with a swarthy
group of muscled black-eyed drummers, when he looks more
like a grammar school teacher with his sensitive and intelligent face. Still, we must do as we are instructed; and in fact
in later weeks Paul bought a *cuíka* and became a dab hand
at it.

The next scene – which is really a travelogue of the Samba
hall: Biggs with the lads; Biggs with the musicians; Biggs
dancing the Samba etc. Now is the dreaded laughing gas.
The tart is now revving up her hips yet again for the take
and loosening her head so much I fear that it will go flying
across the street and end up in one of the fried meat stalls
– a kind of Brazilian *Eraserhead*. ACTION! The tart sprays
us – faked of course – and we are meant to burst into peals
of happy hysterical laughter. At 4 a.m. I am woken from my
trailer for the scene and feel my trunk being transported on
its inevitable journey. Paul is jigging from side to side warming himself up in preparation for the horrendous act – to
laugh on cue. We will fake it and heave, bare our teeth in a
desperate simulation, and leap out into the pissy street. Was
our pittance ever more earned than now?

The actress who has been warming up the entire night
now grabs my hand and sprays the stuff – first on P.F. I
watch his reaction. He fakes it rather well I thought – with
a high spirited '*Whoop*' . . . the kind of whoop Americans are
so fond of using at every opportunity. However this gas is
meant to get you a 'high' . . . and not turn you into a laughing
hyena. I concertina my lungs into a wheeze which I hope

will appear to the spectator like ... 'Gosh I am having so
much fun I can hardly breathe.' And thus the seconds of
humiliation are over and being recorded for all eternity. I
feel my 'report' is being made in heaven and heavy points
are being lost after a valiant beginning. It feels as if everything
I have ever worked for, thought, believed, prayed for, and
stood by, was being dragged along a slimey path of shit.

We return to it and do it again. The second time it is not
so bad and kind of worked in a silly way. Perhaps I am taking
myself too seriously ... We do it yet again ... 'Who is
watching from above as I crush these costly silks into the
courtyard's filth?' As Agamemnon walked his carpet, so did
I that night. As he felt sullied, so did I, as I crushed my
beliefs into the dirt for a small stipend of remuneration. We
burst out of the door again, looking like some idiots and,
as the repetition was dulling my 'awareness', I noticed the
wardrobe lady holding her eyes as if witnessing our apparent
humiliation was too much for her. She was sweating for us!
I couldn't bear anyone watching and even Peter Firth, who
came out for the evening since he was so bored doing
nothing, became another pair of accusing eyes. Paul and I
snatched at anything or clung to anything that might reduce
the degree of shame branded on our heads ... perhaps no
shame to him, but to me. He clung to the girl, snatching her
around the waist, and tried to liven up his sense of being
while I fled 'happily' down the road.

Again!! We go again, and again I tried to keep those cheeks
bunched in joy at 5 a.m. ... The filth of the location was
telling on us as the collected pee of hundreds of people was
intensifying and the foul effluvia rose in the early dawn; and
we, gay people, caroused down the avenue of our humiliation.
The girl was oblivious to it all as she snapped her fingers,
pulled her skirt tighter and higher while I was zonked out
on so much fun. P.F. and I were desperately clinging to
shreds of reality, the way a tooth hangs on to a thread. We
had left a good chess game unfinished in the trailer and
between takes we would both rush to finish it, as if to calm
our minds back even for a few minutes.

We eventually finished another horrid night. The small
army of people went home. No more make-up lady saying
'They're coming close' – as if this was the cue to dab layers
of deadening cake on my face . . . The assistant who wants
to direct her own film and is gaining 'experience'! 'I wanna
make my own films' . . . 'What do you think of Kurosawa?'
I asked . . . 'I don't think I know his work,' the future director
answered. I tear off my clothes like they were the garments
of a leper. Helmut, my driver, comes to life and we drive
back through the dawn streets. We might stop for a final
caiperena at a little café where the hookers hang out, and wait
till it closes at 6 a.m. That's always a good wind down after
a dreary night.

Santa Teresa

Saturday 8 August

Thurs. was a bad day. It rained and C. and I drifted around and I was building up to an evening of more shit and drivel plus a dose of humiliation. Got onto the set, which was a small square in a picturesque area of Rio called Santa Teresa. An old tram car runs through the area and it's cooler here in the hot summer, but only just. There are lots of little cafés and the square we are shooting in is dotted with them. The cafés were filling up as I arrived and I had a dread of prostrating myself before the gawping mob ... Not more laughing gas ... *Pleeeeese!* I foresaw the customers sitting in the cafés and on the pavements watching me in my horrible suit making an ass of myself again, but it was not to be.

Fortunately the previous experience in the Samba club had rather numbed me to it and it wasn't so terrible. We in fact shot the whole thing in a side street, away from the curious mob, and it was relatively painless. It was a continuation of leaving the Samba hall, and the simpering idiot with the 'laughing gas' was still doing her thing. However we now gave up all the hysterical farting about with the gas, this being the end of our journey so to speak, so I just shunted down the hill and watched P.F. making a fool of himself for a change with a recitation of a story about the Angel of Death coming for him while I stare blearily on.

Sweet relief. I threw down two *caiperenas*, which helped to waft me through the night. It's always much easier than you imagine. So the Escola de Samba is over and the horror of those five days when I felt like shit on the shoe of the director. Once an actor said to me that he wanted to be paint on the brush of the director. The dawn blissfully lit up the sky and the whole scene thawed away and dribbled down the drain.

The next day I wanted to show C. the charming little area and couldn't find the place ... as if it didn't exist. My taxi drove around the area for an hour, but it had disappeared. Last night there were two or three little cafés buzzing with life and lit up like a small Montmartre, but when we did eventually find it the whole area was deserted and the cafés were closed. It took the night to transform the square into something magical. I peered into the side street where we were shooting throughout the night, and there was not the slightest trace of all the hectic activity of a film unit. Nothing; as if it had all been a bad dream. The smoke machine and Lech screaming 'More smoke ... Less smoke', and P.F. facing uphill and saying those awful lines with more conviction than they were worth. All gone.

8 August

Had a deep concern whether C. comes to the set to see me work. There's going to be musicians and hundreds of people but I hate being watched when I work by anyone who is intimate to me. I think all actors feel this and never like to know who is 'out front'. Even if there are thousands 'out front' the actor will always ask, 'Was there anyone in tonight?' – that is, after he has finished his show. It's natural since you want to be buried inside the role and a group of strangers is best. A first night is so crowded with people and critics that the overkill practically cures you – as walking on a mass of pebbles is less painful than walking on one. Anyway, that's my feeling; so why disguise it, apologise, feel guilty, or cowardly, or find any other sticks to beat myself with? But everytime the drummers exploded I thought of C. Every sweet Brazilian face or group of costumes swirled into a mass of colours made me think what a pity I am being so precious. In the end I couldn't speak to anyone, so ashamed I was of my cowardice, and when Ronnie Biggs came with his birthday cake I could hardly swallow it. However, each man to his poison.

I have never liked being seen 'working'. People always want to come to the set and actors usually don't say they mind. But inwardly they loathe making a wrong move in front of their lovers or wives or friends. They feel they *ought* to invite them whereas I feel I *don't* ought to. When I am not playing she can come. Sure it may be fun to watch, but I still need to be unconscious of the crowd and need no extra diversions when making a fool of myself – especially in this. If it is a general rule, why break it? I did once feel that, as a player, one should be impervious. But one is not. One need not prove oneself over and above what one has already done. One should rather defend the territory that one has established.

Had to dance like a fiend last night – fortunately in the midst of a crowd. But then the actress playing Rita entered and her breath was as rich as a back alley of a Rio slum, or maybe she had been at the lunch of beans again. Each time she got close I nearly fainted. The *passarela* was exciting at first, with 500 tackily dressed dancers walking in endless circles to those powerful machine-like drummers of the *batteria*. Some wore peacocks' feathers, and others gathered together last year's bits of tat – and I can imagine that on a hot sunny day at the height of the carnival it must all look and feel very exciting, but now, seeing these people parade endlessly in a circle – all the ordinary people of Rio who dress up once a year for a little fantasy – it all looked hopelessly tatty and repetitive. However, the way we work they would be doing many more endless circles.

However, I did what I was requested to do – and that was to stand on my head like an idiot. Like a complete and utter moron I stood on my head, as this seemed to our director to symbolise something about winning or losing some obscure bet. I was very glad C. wasn't there. Only God could see me, and ticked off points.

I went home and counted off the days. It sadly looks like

it is going on with no respite. Still, I now have the joint party with Biggs to look forward to; although I am not relishing it too much. I still have to think that whatever Lech does in this film, at least his whole being is in it and one has hopes. Four down; eight to go.

Monday 10 August

Last night Lech came to my trailer to talk to me. I arrived late. He complained about *my* being difficult, when his shooting is not only indulgent but abuses actors. He wastes them with endless takes until they are rags with no feeling left. He must trust his material more and not work actors till they hate the script, the work, and Brazil. He, no doubt, wants to get the best possible shot and seeks to extract every ounce from a scene. But after a while the results become less good. So he came in the trailer and attempted to mend the breach and was most pleasant. He told me that Macfarland was really 'him'! And how he went to America and studied accountancy so that he could raise his own money to make movies. I quite like that since he is barely into his thirties now. He told me how people warned him that it would take forever, and that everybody talks sweetly but nobody parts with their dough. But he went to see a man who wrote out a cheque for a half million dollars on the spot. He was proud, and the little story was an illustration maybe that my limply written character had to be possessed of the same determination.

So we drank *cachassis* and wallowed on. Suddenly his face became as I knew him earlier, mellowed out and gentler. He claimed admiration for my work etc. So a little thawing eased out the situation, and working wasn't so awful – even if we did have to work until the dreaded 6 a.m. Paradoxically I am getting to like the night shooting, the bar around each corner and the iced *caiperena* and a juicy steak sandwich. The bars, as usual, are real sanctuaries, and around the U-shaped bar we sit, unable to resist comparing the deadened British pub and its dead people playing their ubiquitous slot machines with the welcoming Brazilian bar, with its smells of food and fruit juices, coffee, smoking meat, or just plain beer. But England has a health service which they don't have here; so Britain is a better place to be sick or to die in, but not too good for healthy people to *live* in. Even with all the pain of the film I only have to think of that moribund 'Woganised' Britain to feel, well it's not so bad.

Last night did the scene with the whore Rita. An old house and an interminable time to wait. I plead with Rita to let me in . . . She threatens to call the police . . . I force myself into the room . . . She runs to the window . . . I grab her and pull her away from the window . . . 'No don't do it' . . .

When she struggles and runs to the window the camera's too close to pan at that speed, and loses her for half a second. So she is told to slow down, which is totally against the feeling of the scene for the poor actress. So she has to walk slowly to cry 'Police!' All her real and natural instincts – both correct and spontaneous – are curtailed until she becomes wooden and unresponsive. On 'ACTION' she keeps forgetting, and runs across the room because that's what people do when screaming out for police. But not in this film mister. ACTION: She goes again, and again almost forgets and 'brakes'. So we did the scene endlessly over and over, and I was drained, not because we had to get it right but because we had to get it right all night. Still, it went faster and was better than walking up and down the stairs all night.

I smoked, drank with Peter Firth, and spent the night ruining my system drinking coffee and eating rubbish. The square was an old and rather derelict part of Rio which had a rather decayed charm. It looked vaguely Venetian. Two forlorn figures were sitting at the edge of the square this morning at about 4 a.m. A young man with his head in his hands, and a young woman. Neither had a place to sleep, so they just sat there. I asked Helmut to ask the woman what she was doing there. She replied to him, 'Sitting'. Helmut drove me home and I ordered breakfast on the balcony and watched the light increasing over the sea.

11 August

Last night we had the party at Deitrich's house. Nobody turned up at the magic hour to be able to watch the sun set and have a barb outside. Anyway it was a Monday and the crew had been working all night on Sunday. Ida, who was arranging everything, didn't get there until late and so I was relieved that nobody showed up at an empty house. Biggs arranged some music. We agreed to split the costs, although the musicians' fees seemed a trifle high for Rio. However once it got going people seemed to enjoy it. The place was empty and a straggle of people hung around for some barbecue. Biggs turned up late and it started to roll . . . a bit. My spirit was out of it but I ate some barbecue, danced a bit with C. and got pissed on *caiperena*. P. Free sat in a hammock and played with his beautiful little daughter, and faces gradually swelled the throng. My head started to split and I joined the convoy of busses laid on to take us home. As we headed through the little private wood we saw the director and some others walking up the path to the fast depleting party. We had just made it. Was glad it was all over. And was it worth all that agonising about it? Woke up the next day relieved and hungover. It was all over.

Grumari Beach

50. So far feel O.K. and on top of it, and almost relieved at the same time that I arrived here in one piece. It's so peaceful here, sitting at a white wooden table, which bring me right back to memories of the Greek islands. The thing to do is to take it easy when you can, and today feels soft and warm – sea sounds and the thick green hills of Grumari; something most unspoiled and delightful.

Wednesday 12 August

There's a lot of whores in this area, so one perhaps gets a distinctly exaggerated impression; but perhaps not. I've seen them all over the city, but most here in Copa. At one time every other woman – especially mulatto – seemed to be on the game. One seems to sense that there must be more supply than demand, since the girls are not yet wearing that worn out, sallow look, and seem reasonably 'normal' and fresh looking. As if it's an amateur sport that we can all indulge in. One sees the girls sitting for hours without a client, and nursing one beer, while giving you a determined eye and making all sorts of suggestions with tongue and hand to leave you in no doubt of the services that twenty dollars will buy you. It almost looks innocent – and certainly not vicious or dangerous in the way of the *vice anglaise*. Sometimes they are inclined, if you seem not quite resolute or steadfast, to throw themselves on you, begging and imploring and looking cutely earnest and desperately disappointed if you resist. You almost want to, just to make *them* happy – which of course is what they aim for. Some are young, and many are very young and look exactly like their European counterparts who would be going to work as secretaries or teachers; except here they are going out to rent their bodies. They don't seem to mind too much, and some even seem to take pride in their work.

They parade up and down the Copacabana or work from cafés where they sit all evening in the hope that they may have the doubtful pleasure of earning twenty dollars by shoving someone's strange and unknown tool in their mouths. They don't have too much choice here with a nation that is mostly unemployed and the other half paid absurdly low wages. 42% of Brazil is analphabet. So what does a young, unemployed girl do but go on the game? Or work in sex shows. So this makes Copacabana a very alluring tourist attraction, since tourist dollars are able to reap the fruit of a country that whores out its daughters. The poor education paves the way to whoredom and desperation, and the lack of any health or welfare support further rots ones resolve. Whoredom. That's the way. The state virtually becomes the pimp by default. Unlike their European cousins who do have the possibility of alternatives, but prefer the extra money, these girls have very little alternative.

So the tourists flock to the live sex shows, performed by human animals who will entertain them on stage and off. Or else, if you're a man and therefore don't possess the necessary equipment, you can walk up and down the Copa trying to flog your wares until 4 a.m. At this time I saw several kids still trying to sell their miserable trinkets. One was selling chiclets, and another was trying to sell his last roses before they finally collapsed. The child at least had his cherubic sweetness to help him, and a warm country, and nobody takes too much notice, since there is nothing odd in a child working the streets all night until dawn. The girls buy a rose from him, since one or two may have scored a trick.

The girls are beautiful, sensual, humorous, and affectionate – unlike their frigid, icy British counterparts. Because really these girls are not hookers at all in the sense of a preferred profession. These women have no chance of working anywhere, except in some casual underpaid labour in one of the hotels, and they must be very lucky to get that. I have heard that pathetically many of the women actually hope to date their clients and marry them. Young women just want children and protection like anyone else.

This 'free' society that America upholds and protects so vehemently is a rotting edifice propped up by the military and underwritten by foreign investors. When Castro took over in Cuba he rid the streets of the prostitutes American tourists were so fond of, but he also gave them work and a purpose in their existence. Without any purpose prostitution is a perfectly natural by-product. Despotic régimes whore out their children. It is part of free enterprise.

Saturday 15 August

It's a beautiful morning and I'm not suffering so much. Keep tearing pages out of the script when I have done the scene, but the script never seems to get smaller. Then I took to tearing pages out from all the scenes I was not in, but it still seemed to be pretty hefty. We spend so much time on tiny scenes that will eventually be cut [and of course proved to be cut]. Even the scene I am doing this morning will be cut. The getting up and dressed, and arriving and dressing and learning and concentrating . . . and multiply this by twenty technicians who will also get up and prepare, and producers who will give twenty thousand dollars per day – and this day they could achieve more by burning the money, or giving it to charity. And we will hear 'ACTION!' and concentrate, and the eye of the operator will get sore, and the authorities will have been paid off to use the stadium, and the musicians will turn up and play, and we will all devote a part of our lives to this with utmost care, and if the rushes are not spot-on we will even do the whole thing again – in spite of the fact that it will all be cut.

And why not? You select, when writing a play or painting a picture. You make at least three versions of a script, or more. But writing a script costs only the paper and your patience. Making scenes that you do not use costs you twenty thousand dollars per day; every day. By the time one shoots a film all the revisions should have been done. The final touches to make the rhythm flow and the pace grip. You do not make movies that you will then cut. Not often. And not much. But we will spend endless takes and reversal shots, and endless directions and reshoots, and it will not be in the film. We are working for nothing. But it doesn't matter, you think, since we all get paid. But who wants to work and have it mean nothing? Who wants to struggle, act, create, try to aim for the ultimate shot, the perfect scene, the definitive take, go home satisfied and have a drink. Think about the day and describe it. CUT. CUT OUT. We are working today for nothing. All today's work was cut. I do 7 or 8 takes looking at a building. Yesterday we had about 40 minutes to catch a dawn shot, so after the first take everybody rushes to see the scene on the video – the latest toy of movie making – and continually rewind the shot. This sucks up our valuable time we need to shoot the dawn, and soon the sun will be up. 'The sun will be up soon!' someone cries. It'll be too late.

We go again. I plunge into the blood-warm sea in Urca and – lo and behold – a great yellow smear is pushing its way up into the misty cloud, and soon a painful burning light is crawling over the horizon. Our Orpheus collapsed on the beach, poor man, with exhaustion or heart trouble. He was so lithe in *Orphée Negre*. How mean that we can't stay as young as we are on the screen. The image stays eternally. Shades of D. Gray.

Obsession

I hate this obsession about doing a certain thing: a nude scene in the sea when we jump in. Not for me. And why? Because my work is in its art. I was naked once in one of my own plays and I think I lost the audience and was affected by one of the more gross contaminations of the sixties. I don't regret anything I ever did, but I wanted to be bold and strip to the buff. Awful! I lost my sense of self. I got dragged into the hippie liberation which, while hopeful and healthy, led to some odd excesses. And Greenwich Theatre in the sedate suburbs of the deadlands was no place to express my newfoundland. I can create the most monstrous, intimate – even what many would call obscene – actions on stage by the use of art and skills of language and mime. So to strip to the buff seems not only irrelevant but typical of how the tawdriness of naturalism has asset-stripped the actor of his integrity. The need to convince the all-consuming vegetable which is the mass audience of the reality of a scene.

So I refused to. But I went through a tangle of stupid thoughts about: My body is my own; they hired my acting, and my body expresses nothing. It is what it does that is relevant. Yet I could not rest. What's the big deal? It's dawn on a deserted beach. I'm liberated for God's sake; and yet I could find in my own experience no justification for it. I find film and naturalism so unbelievably trashy with its obsession with the real, and since I never saw Chaplin, Keaton or

Olivier in the buff I was not prepared to sacrifice my hard-won skills for it.

In the end we didn't do it and it was just as well since P. Freeman didn't have to subject himself to being captured and tied up with his willy flapping about. In my play, *Harry's Xmas*, I showed a solitary man in his room taking a crap, wiping his ass and performing the things one does in ones private world. And the audience laughed, since I was miming it, and could then comment even on the way one performs these private moments. But I was using art to express this and it was an honest way of doing it. Lech thought my attitude as I tried to explain it was puritanical – but it is hard to explain to people who are brought up on naturalism and wish to demonstrate the alleged freedoms of the cinema. I'd rather demonstrate my skill.

This morning I asked Jessel, the first assistant, what the rushes were like, and he said that this and that shot were really beautiful. And I started to worry that I have been unjustly condemning the film, and perhaps Lech really has a unique vision and my little journal of agony has maligned what may turn out to be a good movie. I feel a bit like an informer in using the power of my pen to criticise what I am, after all, being paid for. However, I can only write what I feel, and writing is a great releaser of steam. If, in the end, the film turns out to be a masterpiece I will be most happy, but it cannot change the pain of making it. Even Lech seems more patient and less bossy now. He is practically gentle. My own rages at the beginning were an accumulation of his and my nerves on a conflict course – although the handling of the major scenes in the beginning of the film was like an assault course. Maybe as we get to the small scenes things will ease off. False optimism.

Back to the stadium again to watch P.F. play his *cuíka* with the *batteria* while I am spying on him with my binoculars. The shot was set up in three different ways since there didn't seem to be much else to do. Mark's work schedule is, as usual, incredibly lenient. I pick up the binoc. and look three or four times. O.K. Then they lay the favoured railway lines

and I walk into frame. And then the camera stares up my
nostrils while I lean so far over the wall I need two blokes
to hold my legs lest I terminate my young life. What a way
to go! Seven or eight of these. And then the camera goes
upstairs and a long break, and I'm brought back to be seen
climbing up a wall. I like this since it's a bit physical. Four
more of these. I am sure some of these shots will look
good . . . but such an expenditure of film, while the story
waits like the cream in the middle of the cake that you
are nibbling round and never somehow confront. All the
American women attached to the crew hang around with not
much else to do except gossip endlessly. In the end the scene
was cut.

Capoeira Dancers

It's quite amazing. These dancers who combine music, dance
and unarmed combat into an art form the like of which I
have never seen. A legacy of the slave trade when battles
were decided without any mortal blows since, according to
what I've heard, the slave owners were reluctant to see their
slaves – their valued possessions – too damaged for work; so
forbade fighting. Hence *capoeira*. In the street I saw a group
of wonderful lithe young, brown bodies, twisting and weaving
round each other, swinging a scythe-like foot at blurring
speed, cutting the air and missing the opponent's chin by a
hair's breadth. Feet used only; no fists or hands. Sometimes
like monkeys and sometimes like birds, swaying forwards and
backwards, then twisting the body on its axis and letting the
leg be swung through the air; or avoiding the blow by a
remarkable back somersault using just one hand to land on
their feet again, and sometimes achieving a full somersault
or backflip. Totally alert to each other's potentially lethal
assaults, pretending to kick and pulling away just before;
feinting, bobbing, weaving, withdrawing one's head a split
second before a knuckled foot or heel would have made its
painful imprint, and then at the full flow of the move the
attacker whirls into a handstand and kicks backwards so the

body never stops moving and becomes a windmill of limbs, attacking it in all directions.

Dangerous to get too close, and yet they seem to dare the impossible, to bring their bodies so close and just deflect, following each other's moves they become almost mirror images of each other – like cogs – as one strikes and misses, the other is completing his move. They mesh like perfect musical instruments, always in time to the music. As one withdraws, the other attacks. Obeying rhythms of nature or animals: in and out, yin and yang, giving and taking. They seem fearless with full confidence in their lightly muscled but highly defined bodies. Now one actually stands on his head and twists like a break dancer and kicks as he comes out of the spin; and yet all the time we feel these moves are necessary for the battle and are not mere decoration. Thrusting their chests out, now posing like fighting cocks, sometimes almost insect-like. One does a spin on one foot while the other performs a leap that would do credit to Nureyev. Always the music emphasising the action, the same drum and a long stick which resembles a bow and arrow and which is plucked.

Capoeira is a dance fight. How the street breeds the dynamic spirit of its people. Street life. Street games. Street improvisation. The dance of the poor – but how much richer than those who sit in gloomy expensive restaurants, stuffing themselves, while outside their windows are the real princes of the city. Loose, fit, handsome, powerful. We watch in a kind of entranced awe the spectacle, revealing to us the wonderment of man. Exposing our limitations and how unfit we are compared to these young braves.

The poor Brazilians create simple diversions which over the years become more and more complex and dazzling, and are all based on a daring of seeing how far the body can go, of what miracles of speed and defiance it is capable. True theatre. Powerful, risk-taking and awesome to behold. How much more positive than our constipated, neurotic dribble that we pay fortunes to be bored at. Here, for a few gratefully-received pennies we can be treated to what the artist can

really achieve. Sometimes I have seen just two fighters with
their musicians, and tonight there was a whole group, with
two jumping in as the others flag. Downtown in Rio I saw
two amazing dancers who, once they had a captive audience,
stopped and started selling a form of soap, and only returned
to their dance once they had made sufficient sales. The irony
was that their skills, which were so formidable, were only an
excuse to get the crowd so as to peddle some cheap toiletries.
Then, with no less skill than had been used for the fight,
one of them began a sales routine that was no less compelling,
and, though I couldn't understand a word, I was equally
impressed by the power of his voice and delivery and, since
gulfs of laughter swept through the audience, he was a
formidable stand-up comic!

In the group I was watching tonight there was a child of
no more than ten years old who took his place and went
through his motions like a baby veteran, executing incredibly
fast spins, his tiny legs working like pistons. What a training
for such a fledgling. No whingeing in front of the T.V.
for this one, or crying for his toys or other substitute love
accessories, since his parents couldn't afford such absurd
junk. His life was fully expressed here and his strong young
frame was already glistening, and his rewards were the approval of his peers and the claps of his audience.

The strength of performance in street theatre is noticeable
by its absence of the neurotic cries of middle class art. If
there is such a definition of middle-class art it is by its
preoccupation with its own trivialities and its weaknesses
which is then heralded by equally vapid criticism into an art
form. Problems are blown up by minds that have no interest
outside their limited field of activity. The rot that one is left
to witness is the decay caused by the actual blocking up of
the conduits of free expression. Today's theatre stinks of an
amateurism that has no conception of the body language of
the people. It is this very unawareness that is the source
of many of their neuroses in the first place; its rampant
unawareness of the marvellous uses of the body as a tool and
a means of expression counterbalancing the voice. Dance,

martial arts, children's street games, songs, are grist to the mill of the theatre. In L.A. I witnessed the sheer power and audacity of breakdance, with its link back to French mime, its witty and kinetic use of the body compared to the lazy slugs flopping about in discos. If only theatre had some of this daring. What life these dancers had and what sheer vitality. The audience was transported by them and felt better watching them. The sign of good theatre: it makes you feel better. It doesn't make you feel sick.

Rio: The Beachfront
14 August

There is not a lot that is not offered to you as you sit outside a Copacabana café since you will eventually be swarmed by an army of people who walk up and down trying to sell their pathetic wares. The sadness is that it is all so desperate and behind each eager, smiling face there probably sits a family waiting. As you sit you are accosted at all levels as your body presents a potential target for attack. Round your feet, like little mice, are shoeshine boys, cajoling, imploring, pointing out the deficiency of gleam in your white trainers. As these little cherubs are worming their way in, others are sensing you out like mosquitos smelling blood – which is your unspent *cruzeiros* in your pocket. The peanut vendor comes with his cone of peanuts that he heats on his little mobile stove. It's heated with charcoal so he must carry in one hand a bag of charcoal and in the other his little furnace, heating the cones of peanuts on top. So he has quite a preparation. His stove is his life-line and expectation. He carefully fondles it and feeds his little furnace. These small stands are the investment one must make to eke out the tiniest threadbare living. Desperation creates the most ingenious methods of survival. The peanuts are small, hot and tasty and actually go down well with your drink. A symbiosis exists between the waiters and the peddlars since the salty peanuts encourage the booze.

Outside the ferry port which takes you across the bay to Niteroy, a suburb of Rio, a whole line of peanut vendors sit waiting for the thousands of workers to pour through each day. Each woman sits patiently behind her box and sells perhaps a dozen or two at ten pence a cone. This would give them, at the maximum, £2.40 per day or £14.40 for a six day week; then subtract the cost of fuel and nuts. However, when I stood at the ferry I saw none being sold in one hour. Who needs peanuts? Not to the extent that there should be an army of people selling them like they were the last food on earth.

The mobile vendors use a simple but effective selling device: as they pass your table they drop a couple onto your plate and move on to the next table. You automatically chew one and then, as he wends his way back, you feel obliged to fish out 10p. The teaser has worked. While you are chewing someone is holding up a T-shirt. This is overkill reaching a stage of mad desperation. There are thousands of T-shirts on display up and down the whole beach front at Copa, in every style and every hue. Every few yards of pavement is garishly alive with all colour imaginable . . . they look like the work of an insane pavement artist. And yet there will still be those who will drift by with a display over an arm and hold one out in a tired and perfunctory gesture as if they are too sure of the result. It's almost a reflex action by now, and, as they disappear into the darkness, another appears with almost identical items, hoping to catch your eye. Even a momentary dropping of your guard and letting your lazy eye in curiosity seek out the swirl of colour is enough desire on your part to encourage him to pounce and fan that spark of interest. As you turn away, hoping he will disappear, another is on you playing some sweet music on a kind of zither that anyone can play since it is accompanied by some simple sheet music and you simply play the dots. He is playing Chaplin's 'I'll be loving you eternally', which seems to be the eternal hit here.

Ships, crudely carved out of wood with canvas sails, voyage through the air on heads and shoulders – giant affairs that must have taken weeks to make; then beads made out of a plastic material that become luminous when swung and create strange patterns and a weird whistling noise. Brazil is moving through the throng in an open map held stretched out for you, or driving licences stamped with R.I.O. 1987. Meanwhile, tiny children seek to win your heart with their little boxes of chiclets, each child smaller than the next, each pimped out with their boxes by hungry families whose only hope lay in the sweet vulnerability of their youngest. They want only your money and if you say no they ask for the scraps on your plate or the bread in your basket.

Then something obviously made in the *favellas*, those slums that crawl like fungi over the hills in Rio – where the poor live 'they at least have a wonderful view': a ball which is made out of scraps of leather, though it could as easily be rags or even paper, with chicken feathers dyed different colours and tied round the centre of the ball, and you hit it with the palm of your hand and it floats back and forth spinning round and righting itself as the ball reaches your palm and you whack it up. Only the poor could make something like that – you don't *buy* balls!

Earrings and other bits of handmade jewellery displayed by thin artists momentarily take the interest of the women who pick among the twisted strands of silver. Out of the shadows mothers with small babies clinging to them materialise, begging unashamedly. The babies sleep, totally unconcerned with the struggle that is going on. A group of *capoieira* dancers put on a staggering display of martial arts dance; it's stunning and hypnotic and the sweating muscles shine in the dull café lights. At the end they limply pass round a hat, not convinced of their true worth, or not liking the begging bit at the finale. A hand is thrust in front of your face, gripping some tissue which is gently opened to reveal some aquamarines, amethysts, and topaz . . . and other cheap or fake bits of glass. Then more peanuts, and on and on; the never ending tide of people trying to earn something so they can eat. This is not pin money or extras. This is life or death.

Some girls eye me sweetly, sitting at the table the whole night, smoking one cigarette after another . . . waiting. Eyes zone in on you and a man is showing me a little puppet figure that folds up and rolls down your arm as if it were doing somersaults; each vendor searching, hawking, walking, pleading, showing and circling the prey, the braver ones attempting dramatic demonstrations of their toys while the less brave just walk glumly around with their maps and driving plates. Have your photo taken? The hookers wave him off.

A woman passes by with beautiful dolls, elaborately dressed, and when she turns a doll upside down, instead of legs there sprouts another head which shares the same dress, only on the reverse side. What economy! And how enterprising since one doll is white and the other black.

The musician returns with his little zither and dots. He obviously has been down the whole stretch of Copacabana and back. He is still playing 'I'll be loving you eternally' and funnily enough it's still rather a moving tune and I am sure Charlie would have appreciated the tribute – on a teach-yourself zither in Copacabana. Perhaps Charlie's sweet sentimentalism lends itself to being picked out on one finger. Perhaps that's how the old boy composed it.

You think what a waste of human life; what a pathetic nation that can allow itself to be so crushed and humiliated. But then again, when you are born poor you come to accept it as your lot, like endless brothers and sisters, and when you see the gloating and disgusting rich, they are accepted as the natural order of things too. Only education could change it, but who has the time when you would be earning 'peanuts'!

Sunday 16 August

The 'acting' begins. A whole day devoted to a limp, wet little scene that should have been a short morning's work. The indulgence in a few simple scenes as they all turn up, create the set and discuss the whole boring affair as if it were a scene from *Hamlet*! Everybody's running around in the excitement, and the noxious third assistant is telling me to get changed in that humourless voice of hers. Last night we all had a chat round the pool about politics, and I felt that an animated chat about the world is a good way of demonstrating what we all feel without having to do too much about it. We compete to see who has the most conscience whilst ordering '*dos mais per favor*' (two more please).

Yesterday, outside the passarella, I was driving up and down interminably for some reason – though God only knows why and I have given up trying to work it out, I think I keep following Paul Freeman as Biggs. There is no motive for this since I know where he lives and what he does, but I get in the car and follow since that is what you do in films isn't it? Drive. Between takes I spoke to one of the thousands of little brown angels that come round asking for money. I asked him some questions through an interpreter (who was a Belgian racist but owned the American car I was driving). The child seemed pleased to answer all my curiosity about him and told me he was seven and could count up to ten and beyond; revealed that he had three sisters and wanted to be a doctor. How many doctors had he seen in his ghettoes, dealing with the sick and the dead?

Hot Afternoon: 17 August

We were filming 'Rita's Apt. Scene' in some slum in Rio on a Sunday so as to avoid the traffic noise. It was a blazing hot day, and George the cameraman was sweating to see if he could get everything in shot since the room was so small. He was already backed right against the wall and the room was already crowded with the crew bustling around, checking focus with the stand-in, Lech shouting how much longer to get ready and in turn Jessel passing the shout downstairs to the trailer of our Brazilian 'star', who was getting made up. The interminable time that women take to get ready ensures them a perpetual supporting role in the destiny of mankind, and never an equal or leading one. The hours needed on hair and make-up, and base and shading and colouring and eyes, eyebrows, lipsticks, toning, nails and the whole endless paraphernalia. You sit and read or write tranquilly feeling at such times the sheer benefit of not being an actress. And the willing subjugation endured for the possible vague result of looking pretty . . .

So eventually she wobbles onto the set, already exhausted from the two hours it has taken of endless titivating. She looks worse than she did before she started, since now she looks a bit caked up. We run the scene: I knock on the door, enter, and mockingly repeat some words this hooker has said to me in an earlier scene – her trade patter. Soon as I enter the door I have to move left for the camera since this has been 'worked out'; whereas it felt good when I just leaned against the door. This causes you to immediately lose the flow since you are artificially adjusting to the camera whereas the camera should be adjusting to you! The camera runs on a motor, not adrenalin.

It's 100° outside and we are constantly watered by a sweet young gay Brazilian who wafts in and out with drinks or chilled apples. I'm already soaking in the heat caused in part by some 'crisis' which I have now forgotten but which seems to surface whenever one works. We do it a few times, change it a bit and try to render some life into some stale lines. I offer Lech my objection to 'I want to wash your little poo-pah' [sic] since it sounds to me like I'm cleaning the shit from a baby's ass. It's really gross. However Lech is convinced it's a wonderful scene. 'Many people have told me it's a great scene.' He tries to sell it to me by popular approval but agrees to remove the offending line. Instead I offer to 'wash her little boo-boos' ... and I say it cringing in my soul remembering my recent play and the joy of feasting on my own language, and comparing it to this. Lech adds that a prostitute used those very words to him, thus vouching for their authenticity. So whenever we have a crisis over the speaking of some hokum dialogue Lech swears to its authentic derivation.

So we deal with the scene and the poor actress can't remember too much of the dialogue, thus ensuring that we do it at least fifteen times, and Lech wants me at the end to kiss her knee. I hate that. He responds 'It's fantastic to kiss her knee ... Where have you seen that before?' I stare at him in disbelief. That he should find such a routine piece of biz so astounding. He asks me to tell him of any film where someone has kissed a woman's knee. To put an end to it I suddenly grab her foot and suggest kissing that instead, while lifting her leg in the air. He buys that. It means bringing her foot to me rather than stooping to her. Maybe it's easier because I suggested it but it feels better and looks more dramatic.

It works but of course George can't quite get it in frame. It's a simple shot if the camera were further away and much simpler in a studio instead of this chicken coop where we have to stop whenever we hear a car revving nearby. I start to harbour a suspicion now for the knee shot since it drew my stooped figure into frame. George stares down his lens so much he is beginning to get a red circle round his eye. It hurts me to look at it and I have to turn away.

We go again and again and then break for lunch, which is served in what looks like an old garage on the other side of the street. Its ancient roof looks about to collapse on top of us. The heat is oppressive, windless and over a hundred: burning hot Sunday afternoon in a treeless Rio slum. More to pass the time I nibble at the rice and beans and 'pass' on the lumps of greasy chicken in the earthenware bowl. A few veggies and I'm back in my trailer ... my sanctuary from the world. I can't finish the beans, it smells too strong. I realise now why everybody's breath stinks after lunch. I can't even lie down ... it's too hot.

Back after lunch we finish the scene. The bed is replaced in the room and the camera is now behind me. She sits and I kiss her foot and I invent a couple of finishing lines to nail down the scene. L. likes them. I sometimes wear my writer's cap which can be painful but also very useful. I try to kick some life into the scene; after all, I'm here; I may as well do it the best I can. We do nine takes but again George can't quite get it into focus. We pick up in the middle of the scene to avoid the problem. L. is in the next room watching the scene on video.

'Sound' complains he never has enough rehearsal. He's a long, thin Dutchman with curly hair and a gentle face who has lived in Rio for three years. There's always a conflict between picture and sound even if I carry a receiver in my pocket and there is also a boom mike in the room. The constant cry is 'Sound reloading'. L. screams, 'We've only just started, how can he be reloading already?' I suppose Sound didn't want to waste his last piece of reel. Then Camera cries 'Reloading', and then more tape for the video. Each machine chewing up the valuable dollars, take after endless take.

We're getting near the end and I've grabbed Rita's hair for the fifteenth time and, under the layers of laquer, it feels like a broom. The light is beginning to go and it's cooling down. Jessel, the first assistant, screams 'We're losing the light, come on!' His eyes are nearly bright red from strain and he looks like a vampire. He tells me portions of his life between takes and the interminable time it takes to change the set. He starts to come into focus as a human being, rounded and shaded and not just another cog in this machine. Every piece of information vitalises him as if it were a blood transfusion. The film sucks all life, individuality, ego, energy out of him, and so he replaces them by showing he has a life outside the film.

Red-eyed, Jessel shouts at the make-up girl. Wounded, she retreats out of the eye of the camera and sulks. A shadow is cast over her face by some slats and creates the impression of bruising. She threatens, 'I'm getting out of here today'. But at the day's end she is back to her cheerful self. We sweat through the last takes and I constantly refresh my eyes with the deepening sunset scorching the horizon. Cut. Once more. The day's over for me at least and I tear down the stairs and throw off my sopping clothes. The set dissolves and we return the street to the poor. It was one of the most exhausting days of the film. (Later I heard that the scene was cut.)

17 August

Bad night. Feel traitorous suddenly to be writing out my bile and beliefs when the situation has marginally improved; but, at the same time, one mustn't castrate oneself. Stop being controlled by some force that says you must expel each pain

and hate that comes along, then either by punished for not
doing it (cowardice), or doing it (traitorous). So always caught
between two rocky shores. In the end it is best to give vent
and modify at the end.

18 August

Last night read the Buddha's Bible that they leave in the
hotels, and found that it makes great sense and was a source
of relief. It left me feeling that much pain is greed of some
kind. Like my alleged greed to humiliate by confession: to
inform, to reveal. So needing. Then cut it out and leave just
the facts. I suppose it's a basic human need to write everything and put it all in perspective. But then the pain comes
because you feel you mustn't, you can't. Then all is wasted.
No! You have found other ways to put it quite succinctly,
even humorously. Every pain you cause is one that will hurt
you since it is the reverse side of the coin. Don't criticise.
Just point out the differences. How much longer can this go
on!

The waves are high and crashing in today. It's been raining. What do they do in the rain, the endless poor, huddling
on their corners? They at least have one solid wall to their
houses of cardboard, and that's the one they're propped up
against. Walked into town yesterday on my day off and saw
the *capoeira* dancers again. Still selling their soap, their bodies
muscled like gladiators – the finest athletes. One's face:
animalistic, hawk-like nose and thick straight hair brushed
back like a fox. Strong white teeth. A dragon tattooed on his
arm. Enormous power suggested in his agile frame. Daily
they do their work and daily one allows the other to kick him
accidentally and then act 'outraged'. These two young men,
hustling daily for their bread, once again inspire me and
make ridiculous the petty angsts that make me sweat. Their
daily trysts are packed with a force and a meaning that seems
totally absent from my own. Here they can be enormously
proud and know that the crowd hold them in a kind of awe.
I could not claim such a distinction in what I am doing. What

pride in that? Rather shun the eyes of people who look on in curiosity:

An actor's life is one of pain.
'Let's go again' is the director's refrain.
'It was slightly out of focus' the camera whines.
The sweat pours down while your spirit dies.

Sleeping endlessly, as if to make up for the lack of sleep I had for almost two weeks. Back to night shooting tomorrow. O.K. So at least the days are off. The long sleeps have helped my mind, although it didn't hurt to read Buddha. 'If a carpenter has a clear order he sleeps well.' A carpenter somehow who is good is a symbol of Buddha. Every joint must be perfect so as to be able to support its fellow joint: mortice and tenon, dovetail, total unity. Care for your materials. And then the pride of achievement. Are we carpenters, or are we, rather, butchers – hacking our way through the body of the script like demented creatures? Changing, cutting, glueing bits together, enraged with our materials, and using the most blunted of tools. And, most of all, having no clear orders so that we may sleep well. The joy of creation is to make something perfect, since only then will Buddha enter it and bless it.

Feeling weak in my throat when swallowing; so I was really damaged by those endless nights, falling asleep in the trailer with nothing to do, and then being woken up by a shrill American voice. Film rolling inexorably on and there seems no end to it . . . One whole morning on going up some stairs.

Thursday 20 August
early a.m.

Another night of walking up and down uselessly and padding out a wasted evening. The danger is in sleeping between takes, since when I wake up to this I am put in a terrible mood seeing the same old carnival crap and being made again to walk through the crowd, the lost man struggling through the melée of life, looking for I don't know what – and I really don't know, since there seems to be little reason why I am suddenly obsessed with this woman.

So I watched the fat ladies dressed up and pretending to come out of an alley, and I again like some jerk, get caught up with the pageant and the displays. The women start by doing the same song and jogging their hips. And that was O.K. . . . but seeing the makeup girl watching them and lifting her legs up and down to encourage them to do the same, and having had this for an entire week, night after night, made me go into trauma. So I found myself reduced to screaming at Lech that I could not keep doing this shit. But the real reason is that the schedule is so bad that a whole night is dedicated to a few tiny bits of street scene. A few seconds of film. There is no attempt made to ensure work satisfaction, or to balance some acting scenes with all the crowd work – even if it means adjusting the schedule in order to make the actors feel at least like they are using their skills, lest they become corroded and jaded, hopelessly depressed. And so it was seeing all these lackeys around that ignited my powder keg. Lech screams back and attempts no pacification or understanding. Jessel runs after my fleeing figure and consoles and pleads for the sake of the crew and their labour. Not that I would have left the film. Merely the set. Roberto Mann runs over and we are by a tiny run down bar, and Roberto buys me a beer. It's 3 a.m. and the little bar still functions. The beer tastes good since it is mixed with my adrenalin and I feel purged and cleansed of my bile, as if I had vomited out some poison from my system.

Thursday; 11.20 a.m.

The explosion still reverbs. What makes a person who loves work and desires to do the best one can suddenly explode? The pointlessness of it – although it may have great point for the director, and his task is by no means easy – but the amateurism of the planning, so that we nibble the film bit by bit. Then we're asked to extend the schedule which is already over-extended. So the street felt as if I were put into a mad house. I have to walk past a series of images – a brick wall, a gutter, a few faces peering from the gloom – weave in and out of the dancers. Endless tasks. I had forgotten the lessons of Buddha.

La Scala

Thursday 20 August

Went with C. to a tourist Samba show. Plainly awful: a huge amount of flesh and an unbelievable amount of performers, who could not have been paid more than a pittance, even if the place was packed. I have never seen such an amazing and bewildering assortment of costumes in any one show, and thus they live up to the ads the Scala puts into the glossy brochures you find in every hotel reception where you will see two lines of brown bodies somehow descending an endless staircase like a running faucet of flesh. The girls all wear those G-strings with a tiny bit of sequin just covering the danger area. The bum hangs out as usual since there is no restriction there, and the tits are exposed. Wings are worn for their ethereal qualities and to further mystify the female into some exotic, bird-like creature.

They flap their wings as they enter the stage, and then turn, using their wings to conceal their asses and then provocatively reveal them, like a kind of peep-show. The girls jig about as much as their elaborate fortress of costume permits, and, while exposing the maximum, still manage to heap masses on the non-saleable areas – like giant hats and headpieces.

They start the show with a potted history of Brazil, and we see a black man seducing a white woman, thus creating the mulatto. And after his conquest he performs sudden spurts from one end of the stage to another, escaping the wrath of the Portuguese masters. He did this in an imitation of modern dance where this sudden run across the stage followed by an abrupt stop seems a much favoured movement.

The volume was murderously loud as the costumes came

on, smiling and twirling aimlessly in order to show their elaborate and expensive creations while they performed a simple panto of Rioccan street life. Small stalls now appeared and in the meantime there's been a whole costume change for some of them, since their bare asses have now become elegant ladies. So far I have seen at least fifty people on the stage.

At last come the drummers. Not only do they play with this controlled whiplash energy, they also climb on top of each other and form the pyramids that you see in school or army gymnastic teams – and still continue to play. Thin, wiry, sinuous; and a first rate piece of cabaret, which also allows for a further costume change for forty or so dancers in the cramped downstairs dressing rooms. I never understood how they could make their way up the narrow staircase with these vast costumes.

The girls are now back, in more weird and fantastic concoctions, brilliantly coloured, and covered in diamanté and glass, ostrich and peacocks' feathers. They parade and twirl around like birds of paradise, without too much enthusiasm. This is their second show tonight. The audience are enjoying it and knocking back their *caiperenas*. This is a good night out. This is life abroad. A tourist always feels a nightclub is the ultimate good time – a bit naughty, a bit expensive, and a few mates. They feel expansive and at their best. They are being royally entertained and thus are open to suggestion. A nightclub feels 'grown up' . . . something that you spend a lot on but don't mind, since this is your 'rite of passage'. Anything can happen, but never does. The most that can happen is that a beautiful long-legged dancer with a quarter of an inch of ribbon between her thighs will come into the audience and invite Joe Bloggs or Herr Schmidt to heave their great bellies and bald heads onto the stage and perform a Samba in front of the audience – which they willingly do.

But now two very skilled dancer/drummers do amazing things with a saucer-like drum (such as we had in the film), spinning it on a forefinger while doing a complete somersault; then rolling it over their bodies like a wheel, and it travels from one arm across the shoulders and back to the other side, down the arm and caught by the other hand. True vintage cabaret stuff. They disappear and the girls wallpaper a few more minutes away with some frantic tits and ass wobbling, until the bums become just a blur of brown flesh.

Suddenly it stops. The girls are applauded and have a break, and a comedian comes on. Ah, all the ingredients. He seems to be very good and confident, and was given a prominent feature in the brochure, so he must be a well known comic. He gets the audience – by now supine and longing to be 'involved'. We're all just a bunch of happy people, willing to be 'used' . . . teased, threatened with a little gentle humiliation. 'Who is from Paraguay?' he asks. A cheer rings from the table at the back. 'From Bolivia?' . . . a couple of cheers. 'Cuba?' Strangely enough, two middle aged people in the front shout out – must have fled from the Castro regime. 'Japan? Spain? Argentina?' And on each announcement of country the natives shout out their cries of joyful recognition. The whole audience is on red alert, waiting to hear their little identities join the League of Nations. Norway and Portugal sit anxiously preparing their throats for their peals of confirmation that they too belong to the world, while I shudder when he comes to '*Englaaand*' – and I'm quite relieved when two pastel dressed limies shout out in glee.

Clever to capture an audience by zoning in on their origins – the vulnerable zone of who we are. As the claimants identified themselves he rewarded them with a few words in their tongue, and the band would at the same time play a refrain from their national hit tune. So the man has worked out his repertoire of a couple of dozen countries. And it's a big success; especially since the band appears to just brilliantly improvise their tunes. Wonderful stuff. Even Israel is claimed by another middle aged couple, and the whole audience sing along '*Hava Nagila Hava*' . . . testifying to Israel's tough and popular image. I can barely imagine the response to the same question in pre-state Israel. 'Any Jews in the audience?' . . . total silence. A state means you belong. For the English, the band steam away with 'It's a long way to Tipperary'. We did in fact make a feeble squawk on 'England' when we saw that we would not be alone in claiming our patrimony.

Then, having been identified, the various groups who were simply thrilled to be German, English, Bolivian or Cuban, were asked to go on the stage and actually dance their various national dances. The audience entertains itself! Very clever. So each couple in turn climbed awkwardly onto the stage and totally and willingly danced for a couple of moments in front of five hundred people their national current jig. This was the end of the pier. This was Blackpool. Friends of the world oozed together in a big melting goo of chumminess, while the waiters smirked and the dancers giggled behind the curtains. There is nothing an audience will not do if asked. It's being in the spotlight that somehow traps them or frees them. They are released from all restraints and become helpless victims who joyfully assist in the execution of their off-stage personalities. Old fat mums heave their ancient carcasses onto the stage, looking perilously, at times, like beached whales, and proceed to drag their somewhat unwilling male partners. For many this is the first time the spotlight has shone on their lives, and it intoxicates. We all want to be stars for a second.

The English couple now come on. The man – thin and ordinary, decent looking – and the wife with short fluffy hair, take to the stage for a waltz. The man awkwardly propels her like he was driving a lawn-mower, and it's obvious they seldom dance together and he's evidently over-excited. The audience laughs good-naturedly at his maladroitness – the sound of which turns his head and suddenly, in his frenzy of exposure and release, he starts dancing with the comedian! The comedian takes this in good humour, unaware of the secret and conditioned reflexes in the English soul which are being ignited now. It's a little fun, and the wife is left looking eggy. It would appear that the Brits, being naturally a little more reserved than their South American cousins, fall apart a bit at the seams when 'allowed' to let their hair down a trifle. Even as a joke the pattern is there to see. The homo-erotic fantasies of childhood break out under the trauma of exposure. Like the British stag parties on the cross-channel ferries where the blokes feel utterly compelled to walk across the table with only their stinking socks on and scaring the women and children to death. It is not an act of liberation but one of dangerous escapism from the British emotional prison. Such escapes can kill – as we have seen in Belgium recently and tragically. The liberal climate of other nations unhinges the poor British lunatics, accustomed as they are to hide-bound and antiquated laws that restrict simple pleasures.

Anyway, the evening wandered on . . . We drank *cachassis* and we were sent off in the best way possible by the drummers again – who are the club's trump card. And this time there were twenty of them, dressed in bright red costumes in an 18th-century style, with breeches and stockings and large puffy sleeves. They cleared the air in a marvellous display that had your blood racing with its rhythm. This was purer and at least authentic, compared to the commercialised culture we had been forced to swallow earlier. The girls went home to their shanty towns, having climbed into their jeans and sweaters and shed their gossamer wings. Or they went down the Copacabana and supplemented their meagre incomes.

Elevator Boy

Britain seems an oasis of civilisation when compared to this, but only in terms of its government, not in its people, since the Brazilians are alive, sentient, gay, demonstrative, warm hearted and welcoming. But as a government they are the pits and the lowest dregs of civilisation. The governing body so religiously believe in capitalism that they are sick with it. The land stinks of chemicals and the last vestiges of wildlife, the incredible Amazonian jungle, is being lopped off each year in vast, depressing chunks. They are too stupid to realise that if you gave the poor even a pittance they would be buyers and create employment, but, as is the case with many countries ruled by church and state, the teachings of Jesus are just so much hot hair. The more religious a country is, paradoxically, the crueller, more greedy and intolerant they seem to be. The threat of communism is the greatest gift the Church has ever had. Now any evil regime can practice whatever iniquities it chooses as long as it presents itself to be the enemy of Satan. Any atrocity can be justified, any depravity, and wholesale slaughter can be redeemed by a government that holds its own against the commy threat. Merely calling an emergent state that embraces Marxism, a totalitarian, Marxist state, defines you as a good, God-fearing, decent human. The Church and state both benefit from this.

Here is free enterprise at work. An army of people selling peanuts, and another army of deformed, crippled, twisted, hopeless people, whose very hideousness is their meal ticket. I am sure that animals have greater variety of choice in their lives. Animals in the wild hunt, roam, sleep, mate, rear and play and fulfil their animal functions to the limits of their capabilities. As nature intended. The human brain renders any owner of one capable of infinite varieties of function. But here the brain is not of much use. A bit wasted. A terrible waste of millions of brains. Imagine what a civilised nation could do with all this brain power? Here people are enslaved in a morbid, hopeless existence. Even in the Amazonian rain forests the incredible variety of tasks the Indian would undertake in his daily survival – fishing, hunt-ing, weaving etc. – sets him up as an Einstein of possibilities compared to this army of the living dead.

In my hotel, labour being so cheap, they will employ a man to stand in an automatic lift and press the button for you. He takes me up to my floor. I am sure he senses that God created him for better things, and feels humiliated by his lack of human expression. A monkey could press a button. He is a young man, with a very gentle and acceptant air about him. He stares at the buttons and pretends to test them. They are his occupation, he wants me to feel that there is some tiny thing I don't know about the working of the lift, and depresses one or two as if to justify why he is travelling up and down all day. I can't speak to him so I can only say . . . '*Obrigado*'. This man presents endless possibilities of human creativity and is a valuable person to be trained, but since life here is cheap there are no depths to which the bosses will not stoop. If it were possible for a lackey to wipe your ass I am sure they would do it. What future can there be for a young, simple man in this system? The plain answer is, none. Of course there is always prostitution.

Sunday 23 August, Buzios

Magnificent view over bay of Buzios in a small hotel Biblyos, where you sit on a sun-baked terrace overlooking the sea. Swam across the bay once before when Helmut took me here for the day. It was at least two miles, and halfway across I became fearful of the things that might be lurking beneath. The water was warm and I swam easily and lazily across the bay, staring back at the ever widening gap between myself and the café where I dived in. So here I was back again, and I viewed my giant swim with some pride.

C. and I visited a deserted beach where rock pools had caught the receding tide and trapped some skate-like fish. I suddenly saw them as I started into the pool, since they had not quite covered themselves to the human eye. I was even able to stroke my new found friends, and covered them a little becoming rather attached and defensive, whereas in a restaurant I merely would have said 'How delicious'. So one eats what one doesn't know. Sun pours down now like a furnace, and I dive into the sea with my goggles and shout back to C. on the beach of the wonders of the deep.

On Friday last we decided to hire a car and split for Buzios, which has become the Rioccan escape for a long weekend – a kind of middle class yuppie haven with streets lined with small bijou cafés and fashion shops selling multicoloured T-shirts. When we arrived we made our way to a little, charming café right on the beach, with old wicker armchairs and tables that just invited you to sit for the afternoon. So we sat and chatted to the hippy-type owner who clutched a long haired blonde baby and talked of her time

in Europe, and was in fact from France. She talked about
Bagwan, meditation and orgasms and then charged a fortune
for some wine and beer. Then we went to a sushi bar where
we were the only clients, and then went home and crashed
out.

The next day we went for a long walk up the hills and
found a small gorsey area which seemed to attract the largest
butterflies I have ever seen – looking like silk handkerchiefs
that had been blown off a washing line. Then we saw a large
dragonfly with four black circles on its transparent wings.

24 August

Drove all the way back to Rio with the assurance that I would
be needed, and then find out that – with the film's typical
disorganisation – I am not. There had been no doubt, none
whatsoever, that I would be definitely and unquestionably
wanted. So we drove back to find the stupid message '*Not
needed today*'. So we fall into our old habit and sat by a chilly
pool, gratefully being grazed by the odd passer by. Paul F.
joins us and tries to wake us from our lethargy but in the
end gives up. And we then flopped into the Italian restaurant
round the corner and both order two wrong dishes. We
return stuffed and pissed to our hotel where I gratefully
throw myself into bed and read Umberto Eco which I enjoy.
The writing and observation are brilliant and remind me to
devote myself to a more intellectual life in the future and not
do anything that corrupts or tries to corrupt. The challenges
and decisions thrown up by this heap of old socks are trite
and neurotic, and each so-called challenge comes from some
bind I find myself in. Feeling so unpleasant at work I am
reluctant to have C. watch me on the set. This is beginning
to get to me since I feel she is getting bored sitting in the
hotel when it is constantly grey and drizzly; and yet the
decision weighs on me to reach a conclusion. The conclusion
must be to be true to myself. Certainly C. needs more stimu-
lation, even if it does mean a crumb of discomfort for me.
Such are the whiny trivial complaints that nag at me in Brazil.

26 August

Did I ever want to tear the leaves off my branches so desperately? I even check my face in the mirror to catch any signs of ageing or premature ravaging. After this nightmare I want to enjoy my freedom, and I hope I will still be youthful – like a prisoner who counts off the months and years and fervently prays for something as simple and profound as still having his hair when he comes out. To be still attractive. Every day draws inexorably by like a slow moving shadow. I long to shave my head and run along a beach, or even see friends.

Yesterday we did the scene in the doorway when I meet Biggs's wife, and she gets all the inflections wrong since she's Brazilian and now lives in Italy. But she is very sweet and we do the simple scene endlessly. We shot the master* (9 takes). Then a break while we set up the reverse shots, and this takes forever. Then, half-asleep, we do C/U on Lucinda; then Lucinda's eyes ... then another break and we do my C/U. Then C/U on my lips; then Paul's C/U ... and all in all the total tally that night was something like 4,000 feet of film. While no doubt there was a good reason to make the scene inventive and compelling, shooting footage at this rate must cost a fortune. As a rule of thumb, with crummy producers you always get crummy movies. This might be the exception through Lech's inventive eye, but generally producers who are scummy permeate into the very entrails of the work, like slime on old vegetables. The poison eats into the cast and the crew and the make-up and even the food you eat on the set.

A totally dead feeling pervades me, as if I couldn't even feel my own body. No desire, passion, feelings, needs. Just the deadness of the film eating into the soul. However time is moving on. Two/three months of my life. What can I do to absolve myself? Now if I could produce a play, or a

---

*The 'master' is a take of the whole scene, which is used as a reference point to cut away from for close-ups.

significant book . . . A new skill? Somehow the nightmare of all this is the lack of stimulus going into my system.

Thursday 27 August

Last night shot a scene with Macumba offerings, and then a fight with kids on the beach. I quite liked the scene since there was no dialogue and it felt like a silent movie. A guy sees these offerings on the beach – booze, cigs etc. – and decides to try some of the booze. Looks around furtively but can't resist trying it. Like a kid who sees something for free. Also curiosity. I pick up the bottle and swig. It's ghastly. Spit it out and put the bottle down but upset the candles which were lit. I attempt to right the candles and knock over something else – some powdered substance which I also attempt to sweep up – and so it goes on like a chain effect. I split in frustration. The scene was eventually cut.

Before the next scene, which was the fight, I fell asleep, woke, smoked, drank beer. There's something weird about working through the night. There's nothing else to do or see except the things you are made to do, so one does try to invest some skill and it does of course make a great deal of difference to the scene or to the take. Curiously, I feel my 'performance' is, despite everything, actually getting better. George the cameraman actually expects it from me now, and even encourages me to give the scene a twist at the end.

Humiliation

I hold a firm belief that a yardstick of a nation's moral worth is how much they insist on humiliating their people into degrading themselves to earn a buck.

29 August

Back in Buzios. This time we try an understaffed place called L'Hermitage. A quiet terrace backs onto our room, surrounded by small trees. There is hardly anyone here and this seems a nice place to sit, look out at the sea, and think. After our hot ride down I plunged into the sea by just going out of the double doors, climbing over our small wall and onto the beach. But the wind whips around the bay and it's depressingly cool on this side.

Feel better since last night when again I had to thread my way through the carnival like a perpetual moving wallpaper. As usual I had to wait for hours, but this time I remain cool and indifferent. Don't got to bars and twist my stomach up with beers, but sit quietly in my trailer and read some turgid shit by Carl Sagan called *Contact*. Re-arranged the trailer to be more like a bed, so now it's my Aladdin's cave.

The night before last I had a potentially good scene totally fucked up by delivering lines that needed an eyeball contact out of the window while staring through these ubiquitous binoculars. All night long this scene was dragged out until it resembled an old rag. Poor Peter Firth was continually scooped out of the car and I continually assaulted him. But it was never right, even with those improvisational greasings to ease the scene along. I find the scene so banal that I tend to impro on the driftwood at the end, since once you have vomited out the burden of the message there could be a little virgin time at the end when you can add a twist of your own. We dragged the night out until dawn. The pain floated into the ether and wretched, sweaty and exhausted, I crawled back into my hotel like a frightened beast.

30 August

The last night of shooting in Rita's apt. I noticed for some time an empty derelict building opposite – merely the facade standing and half a roof which would topple any day. Now this building was decorated to appear like a club by adding some streamers and some neon. Extras poured into the old filthy hallway, pretending frantic activity and, as usual, I was used as a motive to spur the background. I am still looking for 'Rita' . . . I streamed through with the extras and was poured out again.

Now within the darker recesses of the building and amidst the rubbish which was piled up high on one side I saw living human beings for whom this rat-infested and disease-ridden pit was home. We were only using the entrance but deep within, souls were living with their families. There was of course no light, gas, water, and this was in no sense a squat. It was home for the destitute. They had somehow constructed some form of shelter within this rotting edifice which stank of rot, and even the cats that crawled around the débris looked thin and sick. People were actually living inside a rubbish dump.

A young woman's face appeared in the doorway of the shack as if forbidding me even mentally to comment or acknowledge her plight. One mustn't stare at the abjectness of others. An old man peered out of one room whilst we were filming. It was the only space in the house that had actually survived as a room . . . Some nation. Catholicism, capitalism and military dictatorship. The perfect civilisation since each of the three support each other. Keep having babies: Catholic dogma. The evil of the misery it produces. It adds the groaning weight of its doctrine to the suffering and babies dying in the most appalling conditions. The church anaesthetises the people with a broken figure of Christ. The military protect you against socialism or godless communism, and the vultures continue to feed on your flesh. This is the system we are so desperate to protect.

The sea pours over the beach here in Buzios like a constant white noise rushing in steadily. No big breakers; just a continual hissing, like distant trains roaring through the night. Buzios is a peninsula jutting far out into the sea, so there're lots of little beaches clinging to each side of the arm and each beach has a tiny shack attached to it where a few locals sit all day and drink beer and show you a fish that they hope you will buy. The richer Rioccans stay and play up one end and, like the rich, they all have the same wan and pasty look – whether in Italy, France or Brazil – and the children too look creamy and safe. They have their little beaches which are sheltered from the wind, and sandy, while the poor go on the other side. But all in all it's a pleasant place and feels like a sanctuary.

Walked along the beach past a weird assortment of wild life which the city dweller stares at in fascination. The endless variety of seashells, twisted into spirals or cones, or flat and irridescent. Some thickly lined in hard white shell, and others with whorls like fingerprints – a never ending vision of amazing things that you had never thought about in Rio. Watching the tiny crabs pop into the sand as you walk past and then peek out made me grateful to know there is another life. I saw shells like open purses that close tightly when you touch them; then an abundance of fat-bodied moths with giant wings that the wind seemed to have dragged onto the beach were flapping their helpless sodden wings on the sand. They'd drag one brown wing up from the sand and flap it desperately, and even flap themselves upright when a wave would come crashing in and claw it back into the sea, and then throw it back onto the sand again where the whole process would be repeated.

Taking pity on one I prised up carefully its stuck wing and sheltered it in my hand. Its large swept-back wings trembled in the wind and I felt a bit of a saviour. It was a small miracle sitting there in my hand and I took it out of the wind into the hotel room, still cradling it. Suddenly its tongue shot out and out like a watch spring and it seemed quite content in my hand and starting to tick over once again. And I could just detect its little feet clinging to my palm. It wouldn't leave or attempt to fly off. I felt that I had stepped into the way of fate. Eventually I put it outside our room on the sheltered patio, but it wouldn't leave my hand. And each time I managed to brush it off, since I wished it to perform moth-like functions like sitting – wings flat – on the pavement, it nevertheless crawled back up my arm like a new-found ally. I wondered how conscious it could be and whether my hand was merely a smell that it associated with safety. Eventually I did shake it off.

Later, as I was monitoring the moth's progress, I wondered if I had bungled in my sentimental interference with nature and that the moths go to the sea for a quick death when their time is up. Since I left it on the patio I could see it die slowly. It seemed so content at first and sat on a leaf, but later I saw that it had fallen on its back and was struggling again with its wings. Maybe a slow and unpleasant death, whereas he goes to sea in a relatively fit state. So my well meaning but soppy interference causes the moth more agony, since in its dying it is helpless against an invasion of small ants that bite and feed on its still living body. I did it no favours. The moths struggle with its wings on the wet sand that I had interpreted as a plea for survival was merely a reflex action. I had interfered in a natural process whereby nature takes the aged moths and carries them out to sea. I picked up the poor creature and carried it out to the beach and threw it in the sea. It was nearly dead, but at least let it be quick. A wave drove the moth back to the sand again and I could see it was dead. Just as I was satisfied in this I saw it raise a shattered wing again, and again begin its flapping. Oh *No!* ...

Buzios, p.m.

Later that day we searched for a café and drove to the interior and watched footballers in their local colours playing against an intensely blue sky, and the blue and red of their teams stood out vividly in the sharp, clear air. Drove down dirt roads getting us nowhere, and ended up watching the sun sink in some strange formation of cloud, looking like a fried egg. The wind increased and we found a café to shelter in and watch the fireworks in the sky as the sun tore up and singed the clouds. A young man was playing two or three chords on his guitar while sitting on the end of a jetty. The wind sucked the tinny sound away, so he looked as if he were miming playing, with his bare foot beating out the rhythm. He was obviously serenading the sunset: a Yuppie hippie – since he then got in his car and drove off.

Saw some children, who looked quite comfortably off and spoilt, throw a stick into the sea for a dog that they showed little affection for. They threw the stick as far as they could, but the dog was fit and strong and swam well. But they kept throwing it back and not letting the beast rest, and the tide was getting quite choppy. They wouldn't defeat a strong dog, and in the end he just refused to go in. I hated the kids since I could see nothing but greed and lovelessness in their spoilt pudding faces.

31 August

Getting worse. Stomach continually growling in pain, and voice retreating behind a grunt; and waste disposal system ground to a halt. I feel as if I am in a death-like state. But it's pleasant here, and the breeze wafts in, and I sit and face the absurd emptiness of my life – since I have no feeling for anything and therefore can be attacked in any vulnerable situation. I think the pain has to do with the psychological warfare going on. Two wars: one with the film and one with me. So I'm caught in a double bind.

I wake up with pain and go to bed with it; am in continuous agony and know no end except an end to this film and Rio. There could be a way of making it fun, but the agony of the work militates against it. Whenever you build up enthusiasm for the work – wake up, prepare, train, learn and make decisions – you find yourself doing drek – anticipating scenes with horror. All becomes junk. The junk continues and rots the spirit. But the spirit fights back and wins, asserts itself. And in the end you are in control. But the degrading directions, coupled with the junk dialogue, become a formidable adversary and it is like wrestling with a mound of animated shit. You try to assert yourself, but the more you touch, the more the shit sticks to you. I become more and more astounded at the junk people spew out in their lives – the lack of adventure in language; or rapture. The boring, plodding, day to day exchanges as the actors regurgitate the same old fodder.

Rio.
Thursday 2 September

Had to get up at 5.15 a.m. again, and start to believe that I am in the hands of a lunatic. Perhaps I am not cut out for film and its monstrously simplistic messages. Perhaps all this is normal, or at least not quite – but not as hideous as I make out. I don't think so, since the other actors are not too happy, and they have experienced pretty weird situations.

I lay there in the dark of my bedroom, hardly wishing to move, and my heart packed with hate. I struggled into some clothes and wandered down to the car, where Paul Freeman was already sitting, obediently ready. Well what else could we do? We don't rebel. We just go on accepting these continuous reshoots. In the car I expressed the opinion that there was a sickness that affected all of us, and that the film became a disease which they tried to pass on. But Paul would not give in to my exaggerations.

Of course we got there early and hung around while everybody 'busied' themselves. This time they wanted the camera in the water. So in we went again, with the cameramen in surf suits and the camera encased in a waterproof plastic box. So I entered the water, and it felt warm and cosy; and, as I swam about, the dawn was rising and a bright red sun was just beginning to float out of the sea. Suddenly I felt O.K. and my spirits lifted. The sea was the best tonic from the work. It was an escape.

Biggs was kidnapped, and Bruno didn't suffer a heart attack, as he did last time, although one of the guys strangely split a calf muscle on his way here. I came out of the water wonderfully exhilarated and refreshed. Something wonderful about swimming at dawn as the sun rises. The sea and light seem to penetrate your whole body. A contrast from the waking up!

Saturday 5 September

'And the days dwindle on!' Deep aches in the chest cavity. Like a dying heart.

Sunday 6 September

Now it's pissing down with rain, and the Swiss investor has come to try and infuse some sense into everything. He's a pleasant human being and is trying to give some order to chaos. My little friend helps me, and tries to keep herself busy by taking Samba lessons with Paul Freeman's Samba coach. He comes up to the hotel room and tells us marvellous stories. How to get rid of something bothering you: you shout it into the toilet and then pull the chain and flush it away. He is a black dancer here in Rio and is glad to earn a few bucks. We take our shoes off and shift the table and leap up and down the room for an hour. Very relaxing. Then we have a break, and he sits and smokes and takes a beer or two, and we continue. C. is getting very adept.

If only the script would get thinner. In future, if I have any doubt I will resist. Any doubt whatsoever. No angst and deliberation – just a big *'No'*. The angst I had over reviving *Decadence* at the Wyndhams was about whether I could do it well enough, and it turned out to be the best thing I have done for a long time. *Kvetch* in Israel was a complete waste of time, except as therapy for the actors. My proudest achievement has been *Kvetch* in L.A. in the little theatre in Santa Monica where it has run and run. After this think carefully before you leap. P.F. is free for two weeks, the lucky bastard. Perhaps he won't come back and we can all go home.

Another Hot Afternoon in Rio:

7 September

There was a horrible rumour going round that we were going to do Rita's Apartment Scene again. I swore to Mark Slater, the line producer, that there was no way in the world I would do it. On this film one is certain to be fighting for one's soul on an almost daily basis. The idea of doing all that again was a fate too horrible to contemplate. Eventually, as always, I was persuaded by Lech since he promised to do only one shot that was dark. Rita's mulatto skin disappeared into the background and the shot was useless. It seemed churlish to deny him one shot so off we went once more to the filthy square with the rubbish piled up.

I don't think I had ever seen such human wretchedness in all my life.

We were going to shoot speedily that day since we now knew all the problems from our last painful session. Rita comes on the set and tries to be sexy, which is about as sexy as a Sumo wrestler's jockstrap. A prize piece of miscasting when Brazil has beautiful ladies in abundance and the script calls for a ravishingly sexy woman. Our actress is a charming lady but it will not be long before she is toasting her sixtieth. She is embarrassed by the sexy moves she tried to perform. So, in the filthy room, we go through the gauntlet again. I enter the room and, this time, L. has an 'idea' . . . He wants me to camp it up! He obviously has been thinking about it. The approach is of course quite wrong since it is not only entirely out of character but makes no sense since I am already baiting her by repeating her own words. It should be menacing and have a hint of danger. Cold. Neutral. It's one

131

of those ideas that come out of an overworked or overheated mind.

But L. implored me just to try it. I find it strange when directors employ a highly skilled actor and proceed to tell him how to do a scene, whereas the actor's own radar system will automatically do the work for him and home in to the right targets and make the right decisions. If a director by-passes or interferes with that delicate mechanism born out of years of practice then he is shooting himself in the foot and ruining the possibility of great work.

So we tried it and it felt like overstewed cod and for some reason I am always carrying binoculars – even when I don't need them – so we always have to find a time or place to put the bastard thing down which usually screws up a few more takes. So we did it about eight times. We're lucky to get it in focus since L. has an obsession about moving. We have to be moving into action and the camera is moving and so we're always measuring and re-measuring. The tape is constantly at my nose. Eventually a deadening feeling starts to invade the body as the creative spirit atrophies. The voice seizes up first. You clear your throat. It feels full of feathers.

Lunch break further dilutes and wears you out. Then back to the same room and the same shot. The same one shot that we are re-shooting. Rita is asked to cross the room, but this time is never fast enough! The poor woman can't fly. So again, and yet again. After nine takes he gets fed up and does a pick-up on the last part of the run. Also it means you start on a new slate. When the money-men watch the rushes and see 'take 12' or 13 they start to wonder what's going on and are apt to make certain decisions, which in many movies has meant the removal of the director. Here this is unlikely, but it is wiser to stop and pick up and thus start fresh with take one again; even if it is virtually the same scene.

So we pick up and run for six or seven takes; so in all about sixteen takes. And for what? A run across the room. One could justify this by saying that our director was a perfectionist and no two-take hack . . . However, the hours drone on. It is no use getting excited but retain a Buddhist cool. I resort to looking out of the window and studying the minutely-changing patterns of the clouds. I ask a sympathetic, good-hearted Jessel the word for wank, while at the same time making sure he understands by some simple mime. He tells me it is '*pornietta*'. It's strange to hear for the first time foreign swear words. You try to associate the sound to the action. The Portuguese for fuck is '*forjie*' – pronounced like fudge. It sounds like the action; like mud, sludge, earthy: '*forjie*'. And '*pornietta*' has a light touch, like a flower with its stem of porn.

So, to ease the long, endless repetition, we scurrilously and mutinously swear in Portuguese, and when we hear the sound of 'One more' we say '*Mais pornietta!*' – more wanking. And it's one of those silly things which eases the pain and the Brazilian crew can scarcely contain their laughter at hearing an Englishman swear so eloquently in Portuguese. I then started on all the hard core words until I had picked Jessel clean. Humour greases the way and makes life a bit easier thus preventing conflict.

L. is in the next little room, staring at the video which records the shot simultaneously. I hate those things. They hold everything up while the director goes over the bloody tape, and the video gives a bad impression anyway. So we go again into the familiar routine, focus adjusted, sound tested, the distance measured for the umpteenth time. The actress runs, the sweat pours, and at the finish of the day I doubt if we had more than a minute.

The horrendous poor opposite had no idea of what was going on. The whole area was crumbling into an ooze and nothing was being done to alleviate their situation. We finished suddenly, as if the whole thing had been a game of will and he resigned. You could not use film stock indefinitely and the shot wasn't working. At the sound of 'Wrap' there was a great and spontaneous yelp of joy from everyone – to which I added my throat and once more I tore down those stairs and changed into my nicely fitting dark clothes and headed back to the CPH where my first *caiperena* for several days never tasted so good. I looked round the poolside and the wealthy Rioccans were beginning to drift in while others were finishing off their day of eating and boozing. Across the other side of town others were also eating, in conditions that only the most inhuman government could close their eyes to. The sun set on us both.

The Man on his Knees
A New Symbol for Brazil
7 September

Another endlessly grey day. Yesterday I saw a man walking on his knees. His lower legs seemed to trail uselessly behind him like withered branches where no life flowed. He moved himself along by swinging his body between his hands, which acted as crutches. He was so inured to his plight that his naked knees had no protection and had hardened themselves, just as the toughened bare feet of the poor. So his knees were now his feet, carrying him along the pavement, his view being the legs of the other walkers. He made his way along the rich, store-lined Avenue Copacabana, bobbing between the feet and dodging the traffic, and nobody took much notice; as if it was a familiar and tolerable sight, something you endure and even condone. Poor man should be a lesson in how sinful it is to be so poor and wretched. Somehow it was the man's fault. Nobody seemed horrified or to give him a second glance.

It symbolised Brazil . . . the poor and the crippled reduced to crawling on their knees, literally and metaphorically. His twisted limbs testified to the medical neglect and countries indifference to his malformation. It was an horrific sight. For this was not a fly-ridden suburb of Calcutta or Bombay, or drought-ravaged African state. This was the opulent Copacabana bordering on Ipanema that Sinatra sings so slushingly about in 'The Girl from Ipanema'.

Now Brazil is a huge country, rich in agriculture, mineral wealth, vast companies turning out machinery for world markets. French, American, and most of all German industries

can be seen in nearly every town. It is, in spite of its massive
unemployment, a country capable of some minimal welfare
for its people. But the wealth is concentrated into few hands
and that wealth is quickly transferred to Switzerland, and the
rest can go to Hell. The great companies pay little tax and,
to ensure a certain amount of peace, have a general or two
on the board. Of course no expense is spared for the well
trained and ubiquitous army that is seen almost every time
you take a trip out of Rio, practising their manoeuvres or
taking up the best landscapes and beaches.

Rio's biggest symbol is the figure of Christ that holds out
his stiff, concrete arms to the world beneath him. Never was
a symbol more meaningless. Never did his words mean so
little to those below. Never in my life have I seen so little
charity or compassion in any city where extreme wealth and
unendurable poverty lie side by side. I have seen no equivalent here to 'War on Want' or 'Oxfam' – or any organisation
that could tap some of the enormous wealth rotting in banks.
The man on his knees was an adequate symbol of Brazil.
This is the figure that should be atop the giant hill and on
all the post cards.

9 September

Hot day at last and we took a ferry to Paqueta Island, just
downstream of Rio. We felt we were embarking on a voyage
of discovery. It must have been beautiful years ago: giant old
trees that were planted in squares – or the squares built
around them – centuries ago. The boat arrived at what
appeared to be a Greek island: abundant trees and houses
tucked away behind verdant foilage – some relic of the old
slave days in their opulence – and a pretty harbour. Horses
and buggies standing ready to take you on a trip round the
island and fulfil those fantasies of escape. The dreamy, sleepy
little hamlet, and lazy, long, indolent days; overshadowed
cafés where you sit and drink, the sunlight glinting through
the leaves. It looked sensational, and a complete break from
Rio.

We watched the Nitteroi Bridge drift past us, and sailed down to what was really a short trip, like going to Canvey Island. But the look of it was breathtaking. We headed immediately for the beach, and wondered why the water looked a touch cloudy. We'd seen dolphins, only minutes before, swimming upstream in long graceful leaps, so we thought that out here, maybe ten miles away from Rio, it might be clean. But, on closer examination, we saw that it was a yellow, polluted shade. Nobody was swimming. The island was dead. One or two ventured into the sea up to their calves, but no further. There were no warning notices anywhere, but you could tell. On one beach the entire shore was littered with old rusting cans, and the water so gently licked the shore with its acid tongue. The island was polluted; stuck in a stagnant pond. It was horrific. A dead isle. Nobody dared swim and it was a baking hot day. Can one imagine an idyllic island where nobody dare swim? We were facing the flow of effluence that streamed out of Rio like out of a purulent sore. The stink of industrial rape was everywhere. There was no point in going there again. It was a sorrowful sight. Years ago it must have been pleasant for the Rioccans to come here on their weekends off with the kids, and they must have swam and rowed little boats. The view was nice but I was hot and thirsty and the sea looked so inviting. Poison.

10 September

Still too much left, and we crawl like snails over this film. Took C. to the set at last, and she was fascinated with it and I suddenly felt like a tourist visiting. When I saw the actors coming out of the trailers, complaining as usual, I felt like an outsider. The Brazilian actor came out looking fed up and, in his black outfit, he made a mean and sullen picture. Suddenly the actors looked like heroes going through a struggle, while I was out of the main stream of energy and struggle. I tried not to be in the way of the camera and gently introduced C. to the various bodies. We watched for a while, and then left.

The location was a wide alley between warehouses against which shacks had been erected which leaned against the walls like some filthy growth or mould. People were living and cooking in the shacks, and those who didn't have a shack were sleeping outside on a straw mat with sacking for cover. They slept in the open air and were without problems. Children wandered around and the place looked as if it might be a cauldron of disease.

Stomach very bad last night. Went to Japanese doctor and the sun was out this morning and everything felt good, except the deep pain in my gut that the doctor thought might be an inflamed intestine. Don't know what to do any more when this film finishes, but know what to feel. Get out. Travel. L.A. See people. Be alive. Been dead lately. Probably the deadest ever. Dreaming of past events. Dreaming of the cities that don't exist; the New York that never was; the plays that died, just like the people; two beautiful plays that got contaminated. But I loved the snow. That was good. To walk in the snow and watch the cars slither along 8th Avenue on the way to the Westside Arts Theatre. And then fall into a warm dinner. How thoroughly I rehearsed, with such attention to detail. The wonderful fat Ruth Goteslow; Kurt Fuller, dying with exhaustion as he went over the lines a thousand times for Hy Anzell, who then left the show after the notices were bad. All the work we did for him and with him. All the encouragement the slob needed and sucked from us. The Chelsea Hotel, with its overheated rooms and rotting, gurgling pipes. The bagels and coffee in the early morning from next door.

The Endless Night
Saturday 12 September

The torture continues. The endless night devoted to trivia; tiny scenes that take forever; meaningless; a film that seems obsessed with irrelevant detail. I wait until midnight for my call. I enter a room twenty times and it all depends on whether the curtains billow when I open the door so we go again and again. A whole night's shoot: opening drawers, a suitcase, a few seconds on the phone, a bit of scribbling, and day breaks and we're still there with the infernal binoculars. A minute's work for a whole night of drifting; trying to control my stomach pain, half-asleep, bored, waiting for the morning. And then it comes and I fall into bed for six straight hours.

Every day the same brave crew, the same faces locked together in this painful ceremony. Where so much money is poured away and, like gamblers, the investors are helpless as they see their investment dwindle. And yet they cannot pull out with so much invested. They want to see it completed but don't want to throw away more dough, and so they are trapped. We're all trapped. The money ticking on like a taxi meter; it ticks on while we sit and wait and do endless takes and each one looks remarkably similar to the last. Film is burnt up at a phenomenal rate and 'reloading' is the familiar shout. 'Reloading', always 'reloading' and 'Was it in focus?' And the reply, a little wistful and hoping for another crack at it . . .' It was a little soft'. Always that word . . . 'soft'. Perhaps our struggle is a prelude to a great or stunning work and we are poised on the paintbrush of an erratic but unique voice. Time will tell.

Another scene with Rita . . .

1.30 a.m. Monday 13 September

This is the scene where I first meet 'Rita'. Another horrific night in an appalling scene with a woman who couldn't remember anything but made me do the scene over and over again until some semblance of the scene began to shape up in the cloudy, drunken soup of her brain. Then she strips, as if to tempt me, and what I had to face was this ageing actress with her fat ass and stale breath attempting to turn me on. Now such meanness from me is only the pus from the wound that is in my head after dozens of takes and working all night. She is really a very nice woman, but acting with someone who can never remember her lines means a slow torture to the other person until your antagonist takes on the image of a vampire sucking your very blood. It was hopeless to try and take the whole scene in one master, since on each take if she forgot one thing we had to do the whole take again, rather than salvage what we had. It's quite crazy anyway, since you never use the whole master, but only refer to it in close-up. Lech insisted on doing it, even when it was palpably clear that there was no way she was going to get it. The poor woman spends hours getting made up to look like a dog's dinner, but the effect was utterly hopeless and tragic. She stood there in her female garments of desire, attempting sexiness and producing the entire opposite effect. All sexual organs under such conditions turn into purely areas of evacuation. She had long ago deserted the battlefield of the senses and left only a corpse.

It was not her fault. She was miscast. But this of course gave the director power and control. Each time he shouted '*Cuuuut!*' he was controlling his world. It's a power trip. And

140

yet he was never even angry with her, since he seemed oddly to be enjoying saying 'Marshoom!' (once more), until I was beginning to feel sick, and what was meant to be a slight turn on was the biggest turn off in history. He even made her wiggle her ass, since this gesture obviously denoted full proof sexuality. However she couldn't achieve that first wobble when the two cheeks wobble like two jellies on a plate. Then Lech came out and wobbled his Polish ass. Then Jessel came and wobbled his small starved Brazilian cheeks; and even I had a go. It was something to do with flicking your spine, and all young, lithe, beautiful Samba dancers do it every night.

After we had all demonstrated our pneumatic cheeks the next take was perfect. But she forgot the wiggle of the cheeks! After ten takes we split the scene up into small sections, since she was never going to get it in one, no matter how much Captain Bligh insisted on it. Eventually, and after much footage, we get through a few thousand feet of film and come to the end of the night. I was in pain from the sheer, numbing boredom of repetition, and the thought once more surfaced in my mind of escape – even at this late stage. I even entertained the idea that the director enjoyed the discomfort and agony I was put through by this woman. Perhaps he was using her to whip me. I was beginning to hate this woman, standing there like a dumb beast in her tawdry rags of cheap porn. I had been going through this last section for three hours. It was enough. Every part of her was now an object of undiluted hate. Her body – since her mind caused me such torture – was an object of sickening revulsion. I started, against my better nature, to hate women and never wanted to work with them again. The dawn broke up the awful mess, and I returned to the comforting folds of my own clothes. Dawns are sweet relief.

Friday 14 September

The following night finished scene with hooker, and then Peter Firth came out to act his scene. What a difference.

While the director was mulling in the next room, looking at the video of the previous scenes with the hooker, Pete and I worked it out. We played the scene completely still: just two actors acting, and no wandering onto balconies and playing against the rushing sea or the cars or staring out into the distance never looking at each other; or any other predictable business which would entail cameras being hoisted downstairs to get the up the nostril shot. Pete sat and I stood over him and was conveniently reflected in the mirror at the same time, so we had the reverse shot in one angle.

We tell the story and communicate. We wanted to eschew all the fussy film acting in cars, lifts, gondolas; and just act. The way we used to see in the old Bogart films where the action was the actors' faces. Bogart sits on a desk. A blonde sits on a chair. He takes out a cigarette. That's it. Acting. I never saw Bogie do a scene in a car in my life. They knew the power of tight, crisp dialogue and plot and first rate acting. No cameras dribbling along endless rails and being out of focus because of it. For the first time it felt to us like a movie. The audience get a chance to know who we are. So Pete sat and I hovered over him. It was clear and dynamic. Even the camera crew seemed relieved and seemed to enjoy it. They could be precise, simple, clean. Even Jessel expressed his enthusiasm as if now he could get involved in the drama. The director couldn't say 'Cut' twenty times and keep rushing in from the next room where he watches it on the video. This gives a feeling of activity and a false sense of achievement. Here he could only watch and make the odd suggestion since the scene palpably worked.

I don't think he was too happy. It was too easy and he needed the pain. Here I felt was the nub of the problem. He had to be *seen* directing, and to feel it was all being squeezed out of his hands, as if it were the cream in the pastry cook's bag that is squeezed to make the fancy shapes. With Rita the previous night he had been endlessly directing and suggesting this and that, and we saw more of him than each other. Now was balance. Now there was no 'CUT CUT CUT' or 'Once more', endlessly. We were booked all night for a short scene that took a couple of hours. Pete and I persuaded him to at least once try a simple, classic approach, and he seemed to acccept it but was ambivalent. After we had shot it five or six times Pete Firth said 'All right, we're on the wrong set' – meaning, in movie slang, it's done and over and let's move on. Close ups done. His and mine. No fluffs. Done. In Focus. Finished. But there were a couple of hours left until dawn and it meant that he had nothing to do until then when he was doing a sunrise shot. We were finished. Then he said 'Let's go again and try it on the balcony.' Firth was adamant. 'It's done Lech. That's it.' And so it was ...

The Kisser
1987

The insincere are always kissing each other each time they meet and when they leave, in a kind of meaningless farewell gesture of pursing two greasy red lips and making a sound like a moue. It's perfunctory and so you do it twie, and in some countries they do the bloody thing three times. Our director kissed me three times at Victoria Station after my show. I should have suspected something then. I saw once in Paris a four kiss embrace. One, two, three, four times this stupid looking trendy swung his face round hers like a chicken on heat. Is that where we get the word 'two-faced' from. We are always kissing the two sides of the face. The more affluent or stinking rich kiss each time they take a crap, since they feel that such a lack of honest emotion in their lives, such a real lack of love, needs some outward show – a kind of protecting spoor bestowed upon the cheek. Sometimes the indelible imprint of lipstick conveys your acceptance, and sometimes the stigmata acts as a little bond or devil's compact. Anyway it's a small seal of approval and is meaninglessly thrown about when people enter a room, restaurant, or place where the kisser's presence is felt to be of some importance. It's a dreary, dull gesture, as vacant as the ritual itself, as empty as the kiss-smacking air, and is the

currency of the insincere – so beware. You may find yourself
caught up in this absurd game as if by contamination you
find yourself, to your horror, planting your lips on the powdered and caked desert plane of some stranger's face and,
in return, suffer to hear the other two lips attempting to pull
themselves off the jawbone to render likewise to you ...
You've only just met for God's sake, but your wife or partner
is being kissed by the other man and you glance at the
silent and expectant figure and aim your lips to that rather
uninteresting sight. 'Goodbye darling' ... smack ...' 'It was
wonderful!' ... smack ...

Around the pool at the Copacabana the air is alive with
the sounds of mosquitoes burning on those electric blue
lights they are drawn to; but really it is the sound of lips
pretending to kiss, pretending to be pleased, and nobody
wants to kiss but all obey the ritual since it is the only way
to say I don't hate you, but not that I love you. It really
means I carry no weapons but I want to show you how much
you mean to me, and like the French you can do it as often
as you like. Fakers kiss a lot since it takes no effort and
implies a grace or elegance and is not a working-class or
peasant gesture. Nothing would be more absurd than for a
peasant to bite the air like a dying goldfish.

No. Either a real hug, when you can feel the person's body
and know by how they hold you how much they really mean
to you, or better still, what is more sensitive and knowledge-
able than the hand? What tells us more about someone than
the way he grips your hand? – and it can't be faked; not so
easily. A good, dry grip holding mine can actually make me
feel better. Biggs offers me his big open lion's paw and
crushes mine in it. A hand made strong from years of carpentry and gripping planes and saws; a good, hard, solid hand
and in it I feel the man embracing me. A hand to comfort
you; a hand to grip when in pain or on your death bed.
Imagine getting a puff of wind by your cheek as you slide
out of this world. These women will never know of that
electric charge that a good hand will give you – male or
female – and a good female hand is no less reassuring and

demonstrative. They cannot give their hands because they may give themselves away. A hand is a great betrayer. So they whisk through the world with their sterile pecks and air-smacking lips. So beware of those who like to kiss the air near the region of your ear. They are really the serpent's kisses.

Tuesday 15 September

Got up feeling suddenly that this is hell, and the idea of extending this hell is nigh on unendurable. Somehow last night, when I saw how simple it could all be ... how much time is wasted, and how one takes a complex human spirit and numbs it into mediocrity. A mediocre mind is a dangerous one, and actually affects your health since all options which release the spirit are closed off and the soul has no way of flowing out and renewing itself. Thus it warps inside like rotting garbage. My stomach doesn't heal no matter how many pills I take. My bowels still hardly function without masses of laxatives, and I am becoming so withdrawn I find it difficult to communicate with my colleagues without intense self-consciousness.

The sun was out for the first time yesterday and we lay out on the beach. C. got burnt. Then we went for a sushi which is always nice, and on the way back were again stunned by these black *capoiera* dancers performing their lightning spins with legs like outstretched missiles. In the semi-darkness where they performed we saw the true spirit of Brazil. The true power, beauty, agility and care in not hitting each other. Dedicated like supreme artists. I envied them and felt stale. I gave them some money but wanted to give them everything I had. These are the true jewels of Brazil and not the junk stones in the fancy shops – those cess pits where the rich plonk their fat asses down and buy some anal gratification, while the thousands sleep outside when the store is closed, and piss in the street. I lay in bed, alternately sweating and aching.

The Lighter
Saturday 19 September

Start to get vocal angst as the voice tightens up before the shooting begins and I fear it won't come out. Naturally had argument with director who seems to work out all the moves before you start rehearsing – even if the positions are in contradiction to the spirit of the scene. It was a scene of Macfarland's total dominance over the captured Biggs. He had me sitting on the billiard table, delivering lines in a lethargic position. So we changed it, and it began to work. He can be most accommodating at times, and I think saw reason and that the spontaneity achieved by a rehearsal and a free association leads the character into areas you can't anticipate.

It started to make sense and was going well. It even felt like I was acting again. We shot in the municipal theatre's café which looked like baroque pseudo-Egyptian – something like Odeon 1930. Very ornate. P.F. is on the billiard table in a nice clean pair of white knickers, although he has been in the sea, piled into a dirty truck and dragged in here. Now Lech has a plan to shoot the entire scene in one master, which is impossibly difficult since we have props, drinks etc., and I have also to light a glass of yellow liquor and pretend to drink it and set Peter Firth on fire with it! . . . Of course this is a great opportunity to go all night.

Am reminded of Bligh again. Now if any one of the many things we have to do fails, then we don't pick up – as in a normal film – we start the whole thing over again! I warned him about the folly of that. Since, apart from the actor's nerves, the sustaining of a lot of dialogue, and acting to be screwed up by a prop not functioning is a great wear and

tear on ones energy and is a gross insult to ones work. Props
notoriously fail on film, as we were to learn. However, he
insisted that it all had to be done in one, and reason falls on
obsession like water on stone.

So off we go; get everything right, and the acting is good
and sustained – all the moves accurate and the marks hit just
as the camera gets there. I click the lighter on and it fails to
work. Now anybody even half sane would 'pick up' on the
lighter – spare the actors. However we can go again a few
more times. Jessel fixes the lighter and the prop man tries it
and claims I am not striking it hard enough on the wheel for
it to spark sufficiently. It's an old fashioned lighter which they
believe Macfarland, an authentic Scots, would use. None of
those new fangled gas things for him. We go again, and again
the scene goes well – even better, and I'm concentrating like
mad. I pick up the drink, put my hand in my pocket and
take it out, the camera zooms in and my thumb's flicking
away at the wheel like a demented zombie. And again we go.
And each time we waste the whole scene to the temperament
of the lighter which obviously has a curse put on it by Rita,
'the hooker', in revenge for the other night's labours. It has
become Rita! Everybody now tries the lighter and shows me
that it can work; but not every time. Lech tries it and by now
the whole flotilla of semi-employed people and odds and
sods around the set have tried it. The lighter is now achieving
a kind of hallowed significance. L. gets excited and we don't
even have a spare and can't use another since it has been
seen before.

Firth suggests sagely that I destroy the thing on the next
take since the lighter is becoming Captain Queeg's strawberr-
ies on the Caine Mutiny Court Martial. Each time it fails
the small army gathers round the memento and flick away;
and it works. But on each take – as if it was possessed by an
imp – it simply refuses to go on. Bruno (Black Orpheus) has
his five kids there, and Paul says cynically that the kids
haven't had a go at it yet. But before this can happen we do
the pick-up.

We then move on to Paul Freeman's closeups, and Paul

expresses the opinion – having unwisely seen a rough cut of the first half of the film – that his performance or directions were all wrong. So he refuses to listen to L's directions. L. counters the damning charge with a 'What can I say?' Paul replies, 'Nothing'. The two lads had been the previous night to see a rough cut of the stuff we had shot up until now – as a kind of guide. Mark, the producer, imagined that when we saw what we had done we would all be so entranced and see that our suffering had been worth it after all. I chose wisely not to see it, since I didn't wish to add to my store-house of misery. If it was good, then it would be a pleasant surprise later, but if it was really bad I wouldn't be able to go on. The two went and later could be seen nursing their misery in front of a bottle of Scotch in the hotel bar that night.

C. in fact thought that much of it was very good, and even thought that I came out of it all right. There were ripples of laughter in my scenes from the assembled crew there, and I felt a little better when I heard that, but I didn't want to tempt fate. Perhaps I will come out of this unscathed; and I was always ready to give Lech the benefit of the doubt. I was sure that all this suffering could not be in vain. The trouble is that L. sincerely believes that he is right; believes the script is wonderful; the dialogue marvellous. It could be that the film at the end will surprise us all.

We spent the night doing the short scene and escaped in the drizzly, wet air at 8 a.m. It has rained here non stop for two months. It's a strange film and there appears to be no continuity girl. No one cues the actors, so when someone dries and you call for a line, no one speaks ... A dead silence from the dozens of staff hanging limply around. We finish the morning with a strong confrontation scene between me and Firth. It works well, and even gets a scattered applause. L. feels it was too static. 'The scene was only twenty-four seconds long' we cry.* I return to the hotel

*The applauded scene was eventually cut!

to the same breakfast I have eaten for eleven weeks, and contemplate an Edgar Allan Poe sky – bleak, grey and dark.

The Following Night

When we finished the scene I heard some noise outside my trailer and, as I looked out through the small window, I saw an old lady emptying the garbage bins and searching through the muck. She was filthy and she had no shoes. I shut the window and went back to sleep, waiting for the inevitable call to punishment. I awoke an hour later and still heard the noise. This time a man was going through what the old lady had left. I opened the trailer door and just stared at him, since he was oblivious to me. He had picked through the remains and contented himself with sucking on some melon rinds that had been part of our catering on the set. A population reduced to the behaviour of rats.

22 September

The film is constantly being extended, and now casts its shadow over to October 9th. Originally, we should have finished by now. The contracts are slippery and my agent overlooked a tiny sentence which says that if the film goes over, I waive half my salary! This is adding salt to the wound. I howl at my agent, who claims he overlooked it in haste, and I felt that he shouldn't be allowed to deliver newspapers, let alone contracts involving the lives of human beings. I returned to Dennis Selinger of I.C.M. and felt safe again. One needs to be protected. I even had agents who used to help themselves to my money, but overdid the amount once and was queried by the bank. Good old Nat. West.

Thursday 24 September

Hired car and took off for Parati. Heard we are going to reshoot Corcovado – and so the nightmare continues. So thought, let's get out for a few days. Mark Slater encourages me – 'Jump on a plane', he said, 'Go somewhere'. So I hired a car instead. Need a break, and sun . . . Been washed out and confidence at such a low ebb. Frightened even to meet people lest I block up . . . Need rest desperately, and friends. Strange new disease this . . . this blocked feeling . . . Like a devil is inside me. Everyone is a threat. Must get stronger. Even sweet and gentle Roberto Mann asked us out for dinner one night; and yet I feared it and wanted to tell him of my plight. To be able to confess my feelings and fear, since he was such a gentle and sympathetic fellow who adored his beautiful young wife. I wanted to explain, and seek his tolerance. But in the end we never did go out together, though we talked about it often.

Yesterday I showed Clara the place where we filmed the scene with the lighter, which was now restored to a beautiful restaurant. I am always attracted to the scene of the crime. Now it was full of diners, and was elegant and smelled good and the waiters flew around and the nasty scene was erased.

So we drove for hours in the blinding rain, trying to find the way to Parati and stopping for lunch in a charming, small roadside café. We sat in the café and ordered our food and watched the endless rain like a hideous spell being cast over Rio. A deadly grey with no break in the clouds. I theorised that massive pollution must be the cause. Perhaps it creates a kind of blanket that the sun cannot penetrate. Then along came my meat and creamed potatoes; and C. ate fish. It tasted good on a damp, dreary day. Then we drove past endless islands and hills and the atmosphere, even in the rain, felt clean and pure again. The hills were dense in foliage, and small green islets were dotted everywhere – like small mounds of spinach jutting from the sea. Passed several small towns, and everywhere there were the familiar *favellas* which dotted the countryside picturesquely; until you got close enough to smell the rotting sanitation and human effluvium.

After about four hours of solid driving, arrived in Parati which is about the most extraordinary place I have yet seen. A charming old colonial town that had remained exactly as it was when it was built. It's described as being like a film set and is used for locations when the script needs an authentic piece of history. The old town is roped off and no cars are allowed inside its narrow streets. And so it's completely peaceful and cut off from the outside world, as if one had really gone through a time warp. The narrow, cobbled streets all face down to the sea, and a large white church sits at the end facing onto the quay. This was the colonial administrative centre of Brazil until it was moved to Sao Paolo, and when the H.Q. moved the town had no desire to change, but just went to sleep for a couple of centuries. And now it's been rediscovered. When all the merchants left to follow the soldiers and administrators, the place became a ghost town. And now it exists like a giant museum.

The sordidness of the poverty in Rio can blind one to the virtues of Brazil . . . the little cafés with their hand-made wooden chairs and thick woven table cloths, tiled floors, and welcoming, wholesome smells; the warmth of the eating houses and their care and taste in cooking. The café is like a home: a little bar at one end to have a chat, even if you don't wish to eat but wish to be 'at home' amongst the cooking smells and ambience. Food here is very important. It is a ritual that is taken very seriously. A dish rarely appears with your food on it and a waiter's thumbprint on the side. Here it is presented on a platter, and then carefully transferred, like a precious cargo, spoonful by spoonful onto your plate; the waiter pretending that he is scooping out gold. This goes too far, since the underpaid waiter tends to overgrovel. But the dishes are plentiful and the platters allow you a second portion. Poverty is so intense that a humble waiter's job is an honourable one. Even in the poorest sticks of Brazil, in the cheapest café, the waiter will appear wearing a white grubby shirt and black tie.

We eventually find a beautiful old hotel, and the tension starts to drain from my body. A lovely *pousada* with a garden outside the main building, and a room right off the garden; and a little terrace where you can sit in the twilight and watch the lizards – and drink *caiperenas* of course. What else. Small

lamps light up the centre of the garden and there is no sound
but for the crickets. Peace.

Saturday 25 September

At last, the first blue sky creating a kerchief of clear blue in
the window. Impossible to believe – since a few distant, puffy,
white, whipped-cream clouds linger on the distant hills. At
last it's summer overnight. The grey mournfulness has
receded and left bright clear yellow sunshine. The birds
swoop and soar up high, revealing yellow and black markings.
Walked along a shallow river that winds itself into the mountains, past long grass and bullrushes; and buzzards flap lazily
off as we walk near them, or float on the hot air. They're
always searching, and stretch out their huge black wings,
dipped in brown and flecked with white; or they land on a
roof and just sit, barely moving. Like witches. Saw butterflies
with incredible designs – one different on both sides: the top
side two deep blue eyes, and underneath a black and white
maze, like a figure 88. So the film did me a favour today. I
saw a place I never would have set eyes on, and my spirit
rested.

The film is drawing to an end. In retrospect it will lessen
in its horror, but the truth is that it was and is the most
abysmal film experience I have yet suffered. Some people
know instinctively when to walk. Before even the camera
rolls. T. Stamp knew this when I stepped into his clothes in
Cherry Moon . . . How right he was. What a bundle of narciss-
tic *crap*. Some endure a day or two – the optimists. They
know it's bad; the script stinks. But they are blessed with the
optimism of survival. I can *do* something with it, they say
hopefully . . . until finding themselves trapped behind a
camera they are hardly permitted to change a word.
Especially if the director had a hand in writing it. The first
day is loathsome and thus fulfils every doubt you had before
you left.

A bad movie sends many signals. Something in the wind
tells you. It starting date keeps changing. The text is banal,

but you are used to this in film since I have never read a
movie text that wasn't the biggest drivel – I suppose film
makers are afraid of literature or high definition writing.
Then they turn you into an errand boy – ask you to pick
something up in New York: fair request, but crummy. Your
hotel is *not* prepaid, but they don't warn you. The smell
gets stronger. You arrive and it all feels seedy. You say to
yourself . . . 'Go . . . Get out while you can' . . . Days go
past for acclimatisation and wandering around endless stores
looking for my character's clothes. You're asked to do your
own shopping in London, without any supervision, for your
costume.

The first day arrives and is as loathsome as you expected,
thus fulfilling all your fears. How could it taste different?
You watched the ingredients going in. And yet now you can't
go. The cameras have rolled and the deposit's paid. You
were trapped behind the camera and as soon as the film
sucked your soul onto its virgin reels you had made a marriage for better or worse.

All those endless, monotonous takes. And as the days get
worse you weight it up: how much longer can you stick it
out before going insane, against the cost of reshooting. Your
health versus the money. Your guilt versus yourself. It pro-
gressively gets worse than you believe it could; you are like
a diver who thinks he has reached his limits . . . Are you at
it? Can you go even further? You are stretched to breaking
point. You have kicked in the teeth every value you held
dear, until you have become a toothless, amoral hag. You
consider again walking out. It's strange how one can descend
so easily the ladder from the heights in which one has always
sought to be and climbed with great risk and daring. Those
who have not scaled those dizzy crests and heard the music
which is the cry of a great crowd united in one breath in
your support will not miss it. Those for whom work is money
and pastime will not miss it either. And it's not just the smell
of the grease paint and the roar of the crowd; it is the demand
the crowd makes for you to reveal yourself to your core and
test yourself to your utmost limits. As Erich Freid, the

Austrian writer and philosopher, says. 'I want to be a flame
of my generation'. I never heard it put so well.

You again consider walking out. Cowardice versus investment. 'If only I had done it on the first day' becomes 'if only
I'd done it on the first week'. Which becomes 'Why did I
ever set foot on the plane? Was it South America? Fantasy?
Escape?' When, after arriving, I had to leave the country
again to get work permits outside Brazil and, at the possibility
of yet more medical tests, I refused to get out of bed and
burrowed under the sheets. This was becoming a joke. In a
Manhatten hotel I was given, by the producer's girl friend,
a little bag which contained a small plastic tube I had to
deposit some shit in! They give you a little spoon to go with
it. Now this could have been done when I got to Rio! The
insanity of giving me a bag which implied I would carry a
tiny poop of shit on a Pan Am flight to Rio was merely a
taster to further lunacies. Of course I didn't use it until I
reached Rio and my hotel, but the misinterpretations were
to continue.

One revolts after a while; shouts back – the conditions,
the lack of use of your skills; the constant all-night shoots,
where you spend the time staring out of your trailer or
walking up and down stairs, shouting your lines above an
explosive Samba band. The noise – hideous and continuous;
scenes always played against a background – always to distract, since we are in Rio and must feed the background to
the hungry camera. The calls in the middle of the night; all
night to shoot a scene of mind-crushing banality. It's not the
director's fault altogether. He has to deal with Brazilians and
the English and Polish – plus the logistical complications
which are driving him insane as well as us. I know he means
well and is a creative human being. But the experience is not
there yet to make it flow. So he is breaking his teeth on our
skills, or skulls.

The actors sit in cars and talk rubbish all night, and this
is the part I resist most of all. We're the lowest dregs in this
pic. I envy the dignity of camera operators.

All actors from the stage must feel the banal simplicity of

aping the 'real' . . . they compare the sheer, raw nerves on opening night. And each night after, you brace yourself against the possibility of failure and screw your courage to the sticking place. You feel like a pro; your mind a computer working overtime, judging the house, the mood, your lines, and adjusting your delivery by hair's-breadths. To get on the stage is a holy act, and the more you create one night the more to remember the next night. The relief after. The first drink never tasted so good. Fizzy water tastes like champagne. Everything tastes because you are so alive. Here it is the opposite, You're dying and dead. We repeat until we can no longer taste the dull grey ooze that clichés out of our mouths.

Mind you, film language is famous for its being dull as piss and functional. With turbulent, inventive and exciting language they are all amazed that the audience like it. Film directors love action, cars and trucks: all the detritus of our polluted lives. We sat in endless cars at first. You became as important as the car or building or prop or effect. Unimportant but unfortunately necessary. – 'Was it is focus? . . . Did you get much background?' he asks the cameraman, while you sit, totally ingored – always aware that you are placed in position for what lies behind you: scenic. Mind you, I am getting paid for it – much more than I would ever get on stage – so shut up and stop whingeing!

However, you can't. The money has no meaning against the destruction of your ego. By now it's too late to run out, so you grit your teeth and hang in . . . look for acting 'opportunities' to shake off the heavy pall of the script. But one is usually dampened down, argued out, reasoned against. I saw a comic streak in Macfarland which might have been a way in and created a form for him – a kind of 'Gorbals Street Cop' – and much of it suggested a clumsy oaf, out of his element. No way.

You count the days, the weeks . . . it's endless. A few days' break and it's like a reprieve. Then the night work; the hanging around the trailer and watching the hours slipping down the plug-hole. All film entails hanging about, and that's what you get paid for. At least you can write . . . only so much. You fall asleep and are rudely woken . . . 'You're wanted on the set'. You're only background; wandering through endless streets while the carnival dances aimlessly around you. You go on the set, half asleep, dishevelled, lonely in spirit – like a man using his head as a hammer. 'Oh God, what did I do to deserve such punishment'. I cry out.

Saturday 26 September

Reshot scenes before the stoney, unrelenting figure of Jesus on the Cocorvado. Fortunately, the authorities put a time limit on us and we had to finish by 12 a.m. – which we did. Had we had all day it would have certainly taken all day. The scene felt unfocused in content since we were on the move to show the constantly changing background. But we are now used to it. Later that day did the scene in phone box down town – just by the great viaduct that takes the overloaded tram, with its passengers hanging on like maggots on a piece of meat, from Santa Teresa into the city. There was an old, ornamental fountain which had fallen into disuse and, in the neglected stagnant water that still existed and was fed by the recent rains, could be found those tiny fishes that seem to materialise from nowhere and which you'd try to catch with one of those little nets on a stick in your local park. So these weeny fishes were actually being fed by a down-and-out who, poor as he was, wanted to make some contact and feel he was needed by something. He threw bits of stale bread in the old pond and the fishes seethed around like boiling fat. Animals, fish, birds, are notoriously demo-cratic and loving to the hand that feeds them. An old lady likes to feed the pigeons in the park and they leap and land all over her. They are her little ones, and throng round her legs and arms and the old lady once again feels a source of comfort in knowing how necessary she is.

When I finished that tiny scene some more carnival scenes were required, and some of the crew dressed up as transves-tites with wigs and sarongs, to everybody's amusement but mine. During the day George Moradian, the cameraman, said, 'Steven, you're going to like what you see in this picture.' Somehow the thought flattered me and gave me an instant boost. Up to now I had been able to get through the pic by armouring myself in a kind of deadening resentment to everything to do with it – an awful 'Let's get the thing over with' attitude. The tawdriness demanded a protection. The idea that this could be successful never entered my head. It was a turkey, and my investment no more than a little insurance that this might be seen in a video shop in Dalston one day*, among the rest of the video nasties with tits and bums on the covers – those ghastly, evil shops with row upon row of lurid shit, and the deadly assistants, recommending some foul rubbish . . . 'Yeah, it weren't alf good that . . . it's a friller' . . . I felt positively dirty whenever I went to my local video store. Anyway, I had seen no future beyond that, and then being dubbed into Danish or Swedish – maybe German. Now to be told how good I maybe am (which I doubted) disturbed me. It made me a little nervous about the next take, a bit precious. Perhaps all those terrible things I felt about the director were misguided – even if the treatment of the actors was appalling. Perhaps he is creating some kind of unique film.

Sunday 27 September

Did death scene of Clive being killed by Jose Wilke. Turn up to find that they don't need me for several hours, so I sat in a lovely little park opposite where there was a delightful café for people of the quarter. And so we had lunch and listened to Hans Fleury – an overweight, charming and energetic Swiss producer who is over here to put the house in order. He has been for me a godsend, in that he speaks sense, will not see or allow me to be cheated, and is totally supportive. His red, wide face is supported by a thick bull neck, and he laughs a lot at the antics of this film, when he

*The prophecy turned out to be true. My first view of the film was rented from a video shop in Commercial Road, in the East End.

is not weeping. He was talking about the Amazon where he had just spent three days, and it is a place I promised myself to see before I leave here – the last wild space on earth – before it is gradually eaten away by Mcdonalds and Burger King who need vast tracks of land for a world turned on to burgers which demand huge grazing areas. The poor rain forests are chewed up by man's greed at a phenomenal rate, and will never be the same again. The encroachment and desecration is allowed by the bum, President Sarney and his cronies who run that pisshole. You would even think that a leader would be proud to preserve one of the last mysteries of the world, but it is being destroyed at the rate of a country the size of Belgium each year. I read that somewhere and wondered just how many times Belgium could fit into Amazonia.

Eventually I called in to rehearse and we did a shot of me pointing a gun inside Clive's mouth. How subtle. Eventually Jose turns up hours late, since he has problems with this film. Wilke is a rather lean and wickedly funny Brazilian actor with a thin frame and deep voice box. He shoved the knife into Clive like a true pro . . . like it was a filthy sexual act, or like a man who had eaten too much crab. Years ago in L.A. on Santa Monica pier I saw crabs and lobsters writhing around inside a big tank and was fascinated with these amazing forms and their long, weird antennae – like creatures from another planet. So this fish café would allow you to pick your dinner before you ate it. I saw a man get up from the table with a pale yellow sweaty face, as if he'd indulged in some disgusting act. He'd eaten more than he could cope with. So Wilke for a second looked like that man. Yellow and venomous.

Wilke had refused to work unless he was paid in advance, so Hans went to get a bag of money. Until then, we shot the scene every which way, and Peter Firth executed his death scene very convincingly while uttering the biggest twaddle I have ever heard. We catch him in bed with a woman and, in the fight, the woman's wig comes off revealing a lithe young bloke. I think Peter Firth had the idea to make him gay, though for what reason I cannot be quite sure; but it had a good pay off here and he had some acting to do.

The director paid me some compliments about my acting and then he gave me a couple of notes which were fairly accurate. An unfortunate by-product of being an actor is that your passivity means that you are a lowly thing upon which every shadow is felt. Your body and mind are merely recipients or receptacles for others' ideas, and you open your legs or your head and let your mind be screwed. You live only in the eyes of your creator. What's Lech feel today? What's he decided to reshoot? Are we going to Angra dos Reis? Your very passivity leads you to be a spittoon, and naturally you focus on the director as the source of pain, pleasure, satisfaction, joy. To some actors – and particularly actresses – the director can be like a god, a father figure, mentor, guardian, inspiration. 'He got a performance out of me I never thought I had', is often heard from breathy actresses. But this is not unnatural in the context of male/female relationships which already have an ease of familiarity. So vulnerable is the poor actor that a little smile from the director, or a pat on the head – a 'Well done' – fills the poor lapdog with glowing pleasure. In the theatre I work with actors in a collaboration, seeking their inspiration and ideas which I then try to fuse. It's not a kowtowing, ass-licking, overawed, genuflecting business. Anyway, Lech paid me a compliment and, in spite of all, I felt my Pavlovian reflexes experience pleasure after the pain and I felt benign towards him and thought, well he's only human after all and he does have a vision – which is more than one can say about most directors who may have nice easy relationships and churn out garbage.

Monday 28 September

Only two weeks to go. As it was a hot day, drove to the little town of Pedra on the coast, and went into this world famous restaurant which was really charming, old Victorian type place, like a French brasserie. We sat and contemplated the fact that, retrospectively, time had flown. It's been three months and C. coming here had aided my sanity no end. The three months seem to have vanished in a totally meaningless smear. Did little; saw few people, and mostly worked. Which is, after all, what I am here for, and most of my observations have been from work. Still, Rio has many attractions, in spite of grinding poverty and desperation. The people are good natured and warm and you feel good just going down the street and watching everybody enjoy themselves in cafés and dance halls. The beaches are always lively, and everybody plays some game or other; and when the weather is good, the whole country bathes in a golden, luxurious haze. You only have to go a few miles outside the city to be in glorious rolling green valleys and densely packed vegetation.

On the way back from Pedra saw a typical offering to the spirits: Macumba. There was a small cloth on the side of the road on which lay some food, bottles of beer and a recently decapitated dog that looked like it had been chopped with a machete. The pieces were lying all over the road, along with broken glass from the bottles since they tended to place their sordid oblations by the side of busy roads. We will be going to Angra dos Reis tomorrow, and that will mean staying all together in the hotel with the entire crew and actors, and not have the benefit of leaving at the end of the day to go home. It will be a good social exercise. I have images of going into the restaurant and wondering where to sit and at whose table I will be least desirable ... Five days! C. is staying in Rio.

Tuesday 29 September

After a pleasant drive down yesterday I booked into the hotel – which was more a kind of pleasure resort, with lots of different houses and chalets, plus the main hotel in which we all stayed. I looked into my room, which had a small balcony facing the sea, and a wonderful view of the surrounding hills. I shall now enjoy my solitude: now we are all together but separated, and no C. to soften the blow. What blow? Suddenly I felt extremely isolated and rang the actors. I was beginning to panic and was sure that the other two were already making arrangements and excluding me. I walked up and down the corridors and outside in the terrace café. I sat alone and had a drink, and had to buy those infernal beads which resorts like Club Mediterrannée use and which pay for your extras. So I bought rows of those stupid beads and saw that most people wore them around their necks for convenience; and when I first saw them I thought they were necklaces made from seeds. I put my necklaces in my shoulder bag, but after a while got tired of opening my bag and rummaging around and I too walked around like an ancient hippy.

The crew were just beginning now to filter in and sit together at tables, talking Portuguese. I felt very out of it and conspicuously lonely and unpopular, although the crew always invited me to sit with them – which I did until I got bored listening to Portuguese. I rang one of the actors in desperation. Unaware, of course, that I was getting into any particular state, or else preoccupied, he answered that he was 'just sorting things out'. Not even a whisper of 'Why don't you come up and join us?' I expect we all have had enough of each other over the past three months in one way or another. And here we are; thrown together. How will I get through these awful evenings? At least the Brazilians have each other. Then I will have myself. I had depended so heavily on C.; still, I was determined to mix a bit and get to know the Brazilian crew and actors – like José Wilke and Brenno. Then there is Jessel, George the cameraman, and his brother. I will survive.

I went back to the terrace bar and ordered another *caiperena* and sat and tried not to drink it too quickly. I kept bumping into one of the Polish producers – a slim, smart guy in designer jeans who was organising the whole movie like a military operation, and I wondered if he was witnessing my growing panic or saw why I kept walking about the corridors.

Went back to the hotel reception and asked for the room

number of the other actor – which seemed to take an age –
and just then the Polish producer walked past yet again and
I became aware of him being very busy at the desk, sorting
out rooms for the crew. I rang Peter Firth's room, thinking
perhaps we could have a drink on the terrace. No answer. I
knew he had left Rio so must have arrived, and therefore he
was with the other actor. I was left out! I was sure of it. This
was to be the pattern and I would see myself like a wandering
Jew, clawing at the walls.

As it so happens, Peter had not arrived yet and Paul had
his friends over. I was allowing myself to disintegrate since
I had so little ego left. It was only C. that had helped me
hold whatever I had together, and now that she wasn't here
I was in danger of falling apart. Ah! I had cable T.V. Eureka!
That would stave off some agony and I could measure out
the time it took to eat dinner, taking it real slow. An hour
for my journal, and then a movie on cable. It was good that
I should relate more to my Brazilian cohorts. I dived back
into my room and sat on the balcony and wrote for a while.

A giant basket of fruit materialised, and I nibbled at it. I
heard voices beneath my balcony; and laughter. They were
all having a good time. The bastards. I went down to dinner
– which was a good self-service buffet – and spied Jessel and
made a B-line for him. Good! I was O.K. on my first night.
He talked about the film he wanted to make, but I wasn't
paying too much attention to his desires to make films about
rock and roll. I was just trying to recover myself and be who
I was; whoever that is.

So we ate and talked in a waffly sort of way – when the
crew are released from the ordeals of this film and find there
are only fag ends of energy left. Most good chat is done
under the constraints of work. In those few minutes between
takes there can be some very open and real spurts of communication. But now in the restaurant, in the first meal we
have eaten together in three months, we are awkward, as if
we have just met. We talked about making a film of my play
Greek and fooled around with the casting – Tina Turner for

the Sphinx, Meryl Streep for the Mum etc. It's good to make
lists of your future projects.

I sat on my balcony later, listening to the light trickle of the
water seeping in. All looks so sweet and peaceful. Relaxing a
bit more now; letting the thoughts stray to the surface. Wish
someone here could play chess. Glad of my newly found
independence. The evenings will pass quietly and at last I
can watch the odd movie. The first one I saw was the Stallone
rubbish *Night Hawks* . . . junk yard of pollution with Rutger
Hauer. We are all waiting to see if José Wilke will turn up
for filming tomorrow. All depends on him. Some bum movie
when all is geared to this small part. His contract expired
and he didn't want to continue. Who can blame him? So
now we all wait to see if he will make the trip from Sao Paulo
to complete his scenes.

Angra: 6 p.m.

Today we sat on the beach, waiting for José. The cry became,
'Will he come?' And 'How many hours is the drive from Sao
Paulo?' We sat on the beach doing nothing, pissing away
$20,000 per day, minimum. So, rather than rewrite the scene
in order to finish the picture, we all sit on the beach and
stare at the sea. José Wilke susses how to treat the company.
José is a star of sorts in Brazil and has a strong temperament
and hates to be buggered about. And so now he turns up
when he can be bothered. As far as he's concerned, the
movie for him is finished. His dates have overrun and he's
onto the next job.

People have other lives than this movie. So I suggest to
Lech, don't let the tail wag the dog – have him 'killed off',
change the scene . . . anything. But finish the pic. But this
attitude is too revolutionary to a mind trained in the eastern
block. I sense there is a lack of flexibility (joke) and that we
will all sit on the beach until he arrives. P. Firth has the right
stoical idea. Don't get involved, and leave on October 10th
– which is when we're booked to. No more extensions. No
matter what happens, go. Leave the set. Finish. I admire his

resolution and must emulate him. The younger actors have a certain non-confrontational and determined way of doing things. We older war-horses slog on to the bitter end, and then have a blazing battle. No; better to establish your terrain from the beginning; calmly. Here they are, bending over backwards to kiss Wilke's ass, since they know he controls them. So we sit and shoot nothing; go for swims. And Julie, Lech's woman, says 'He assured us he will be here' – as if the whole film depended on a small part actor. The whole two million dollars, all our work . . . future hopes, profits or loss for the investors, labour of technicians, time and energy . . . all on whether Wilke turns up.

He just arrived . . . It's one p.m. Maybe now we can shoot.

Angra: 6 p.m. Wednesday 30 September

Back on the terrace . . . So peaceful to sit here quietly and hear the birds by the tranquil bay after work. There is nothing like working to make you appreciate everything that much more keenly – even if the rot of the work means that you are placed in the mind of someone else, rather like a puppet whose strings are sewn into the brain of the puppet master. The more confusion there is, and the more turmoil, the more one is tossed and turned on a drunken boat. Now I have been released, and I feel free and tranquil. So calm. Just the silent islands and the purity of nature which, compared to man, is the most beautiful thing on earth.

When I see the filth that man creates . . . his lunatic nuclear plants . . . his sheer evil . . . and maladroitness, compared to these islands, the sea, the sky, wind, sun, fish, tides, birds, trees, all work in perfect coordination and sympathy with each other. They are all perfect Marxists. Only humans make plants wilt, people suffer, starve, and develop disease; pollute, exploit and grow fat. I'm reading *The Day after World War Three* by Edward Zuckerman. Nothing can suggest a world in the state of total insanity more than that horrific tale of preparation for the apocalypse. Actually I fear the Russians less and less. I only fear those with no ideology –

those whose lives are so enriched by battening on others that they fear the lessening of their life-style. Those crazy criminals Nixon and Reagan are the ones to fear. Reagan is still spouting the word 'God' as if the speaking of it endowed him with some real purity, the way a whore puts perfume on to cover the stink.

3.20 p.m. 1 October: Beach

Still hanging around . . . always waiting . . . never getting on with things. Jessel calls everyone, 'It's a long scene with action'. The sky is grey and overcast and we're out at an idyllic beach which could only be reached by walking down a steep hill through a wooded glade full of butterflies.

Then we get onto the deserted beach. The crew and equipment come by boat from the hotel. So we sit around, waiting for the sun. I make chat so small it would slip throught the eye of a needle. After three months I make the discovery that the cameraman and lighting man are brothers! I had asked him if he had worked with George before. 'He's my brother', Danny replied. It shows how shut off I have become. I don't even know most of their names. Some actors are good at this and make a point of being popular. After a day they are calling each hairdresser and driver, tea-boy and focus puller by their Christian names. I often don't know them until the last day of shoot.

6 p.m.

Sitting quietly alone as usual with my *caiperena*. I like this really since I can scribble. Had to swim clothed in the sea. Strange sensation. At first the clothes hold you up, and then gradually pull you down. I thought of Ophelia and now I could believe that she floated when I never did before. I felt really free, swimming and fooling around. The sea was warm and friendly, like a bath. Weird shapes of insects; and then saw a large beauty of a butterfly with a silhouette of Australia on its back.

Dinner with Breno (*Black Orpheus*); sweet, big gentle man – always smiling and father of ten children . . . two wives. Misses his woman who will come later this week. Feels totally melancholic without her, for that is how love is between a man and a woman. He's 56 and it's 28 years since I saw *Orphée Negre* at a little cinema in Marble Arch, and Breno still carries that role and film with him as the central light of his life; something that illuminates his being like a giant battery. How he loved Marcel Camus who cast him, and even learned French for him. I speak to him in my halting French and we eat dinner together with the other Bruno who plays – or tries to – a 'heavy', and with Peter F. I'm actually glad to talk to the Brazilians and learn more about them. We are all thrust together in this mini hell which is the nightly verandah, and some idiot employed to play an awful, hideous and amplified guitar.

Went upstairs to my room and watched *Britannia Hospital* – which was quite the biggest waste of time I ever saw. A satire with limp, soggy arrows. Some amusing set pieces. So British and so wide off the mark – a kind of thinking man's 'Carry On'; though nice to see Graham Crowden being so splendidly efficient, and the late great Leonard Rossiter. It started off as 'I'm alright Jack' and ended up, via Buñuel, as Hammer House of Horrors.

I return downstairs and the two Brunos are still there. One can't move with his bad heart (Orpheus) and the other bust a tendon and can do nothing but walk in plaster and so is virtually an extra. I hear about the awful life he spent at the 'Oval House' – a fringe theatre in London. The rest is silence.

Friday 2 October: Rain

The longer I stay, the worse it gets. Drawing to the end the film seems perversely inclined to stretch itself out; like a bad relationship. The day we sat all morning on the beach doing nothing, waiting for Wilke, when there were other scenes we could have shot. Valuable hours, valuable actors drip, drip away. And now the rains have come and we can't work. And again we sit around, endlessly waiting, for glimpses of blue to peep through.

A special effects man has arrived from L.A. to paint the battleship on the horizon which is to take Biggs back to Blighty. He is not slow to inform us that he was 'warned about the enterprise'. He shoots the scene and, miraculously, will add a battleship to an empty horizon. Yesterday we were being shot getting out of the sea, and I had to swim with my shoes on and trousers and even shirt and tie, since they had to be used in the next shot for continuity! Even if the shoes and trousers would have almost surely guaranteed my demise and helped to drag me down, I had to remember to keep them on. I had already been filmed wearing them in a subsequent shot; plus shirt and tie. So I collapse on the beach after our boat has been scuppered, having pretended to have swum a mile, and still wearing my famous Gucci slipon shoes and horrible Dior tie. Fortunately I didn't have to keep my jacket on and let it slip off and sink to the bottom where now, in a remote part of Brazil, it slowly rots away at the bottom of the sea. So we did the scene a few times, all standing around in cold wet clothes; then being dried off and soaked again; then interminable discussions; then back; again and again.

I dream of the times I was a real actor. A stage actor. This is what happens to those who wish to be in film. See the effect film has on actors. Brando, who was a great stage actor, did four major films – then should have returned to the stage. But, understandably such actors don't wish to perform 8 times a week for up to six months to earn the investors' money back. So they allow themselves to be used up in film. For those who are the creatures of film there is only gain. But for those who have the great skills of live performance it is a terrible loss: Brando, Burton, O'Toole, Finney, etc. etc. . . .

It could rain for yonks.

Rained all day:

To sit in solemn silence in a dull dark dock
In a pestilential prison with a life long lock.

Played chess with Paul's driver and beat him. But he played
well enough to give me a good brain wash. So low has been
my social life here that the game was the highlight of my
stay; the most excitement I've had since I arrived. A terrible
confession. Just to be able to *play* and use my mind.

We are called out again, since the rain is clearing. The
islands now lay in a misty shroud and the sky looks as if it
has plenty of rain left for us. Paul Freeman stalks around
with his 'family group' – some nice, friendly people from the
States; and Peter Firth sits alone. It is the same everywhere.
People seem reluctant to drop their barriers and be. So much
privacy and fear – including, no doubt, mine. The film takes
a lot of our social behaviour away. We have little to say any
more and we are tired of complaining to each other. We all
want out, and I haven't even seen the small edited version
which so depressed them. I remember the little clique that
broke off in *War and Rememberance* that I shot last year in
Europe. I, as 'Hitler', found myself associating with crazy
Goering and friendly Goebbels – while the 'others', who
were against me, – the Generals, like Peter Vaughan, Jeremy
Kemp – went their way. But they were, to a man, friendly,
sociable beings. There were more of us then, which helped.
Here we are three. Of course we are all individuals, but there
are not enough to create that mix; even if a little brotherly
love, caring and interest wouldn't go far astray. Yet in some
way I place the blame on the film. It has soured us.

There was a personality split-off even when we toured
Europe with the *Hamlet* team. Politically influenced, we
called ourselves the wets . . . and I forget the other name,
but they were the carousers and the provokers. I didn't know
what team I was in, but certainly didn't think I would be in
the 'wets' since I was directing and playing Hamlet. The
heavies would get pissed and the wets would visit museums
and have dinner together and talk. In the end I decided I
must be a wet. I'm happier in the end with gentle people,

for these have the most real inner strength, while the others
have the macho armoury or lunacy, which is a kind of escape
in itself; a way of taking introspection to its limits. So everybody splinters off to where they get the best reflections – so
you take your mirror with you in the shape of your friends,
mate, whatever. But in *Hamlet* I liked them all. Though some
more than others.

Been here now three months, and never in my life felt so
unlived, so untested and untried. The first day is so clear in
my mind, and the rest merely a sordid repetition of it. Not
an auspicious fiftieth.

Moan:

It's as if I were totally alone here. It grinds away at the spirit.
I even eat lunch for the warm comfort of a meal. My highlight: the game of chess with Paul Freeman's driver. However
I found, by some weird and strange miracle, a translation of
Gogol's *Dead Souls*, and it has been my most constant com-
panion and friend. I had never read it before and am
astounded at the sheer brilliance of Gogol's descriptions of
Russian life in the last century. I can almost smell the tiny
villages and the rotting old farmhouses and the stink of the
peasants.

So I read and read and write and write. A book will emerge
from this so it can't have all been a waste. I'm drifting away
from acting and actors. I realise that I'm in the wrong business and that I can no longer relate to their needs. I have
been a writer of sorts too long, and even directing gives you
an objectivity that acting denies. As an actor you are forced
to be a kind of puppet that has subjected its personality to
others. For many actors there exists nothing but a need to
fill that empty space, since the soul has been hocked, with
whatever junk you can stuff in its place. No wonder so many
actors turn to booze, drugs, sexual indulgence and prattle.
Anything to fill the void. Most actors became thespians
because of some great driving ambition, and were fuelled as
young fledglings by the desire to be Hamlet or Cyrano. The

desire to dedicate oneself to the greatest possible feats of human imagination and endurance; to be emotional and vocal athletes, stunning the world with interpretations of the great dramatic poets. After leaving the drama schools they found that what they were doing was West End revivals in rep. Still, it's work and you learn your craft and, if you don't get into one of the two 'classic' companies, you might find yourself doing the odd 'telly'. But still, the back of your mind is harbouring the idea of eventual greatness as Richard the Third. The compromises are crushing you into identikit situations and you are cast as heavies. You hardly ever do plays now, but may end up in a worthy BBC boring classic where they get all the old costumes out, or you may, if you are lucky, end up in *EastEnders*. Forget your acting the great roles. Forget Macbeth and Othello. A dream. End up in the pub.

3 October

It's raining again! I have already voiced my opinion to the director that in all likelihood it would rain today, and that the only option is to get back to Rio where at least one could shoot the interiors. So what if you waste a day getting back to Rio? Here we are, wasting *days*, sitting here, playing draughts. (Besides which, I was bored out of my mind and dying to get back to a little company.) 'No', they all whimpered. 'The experts say it will be fine tomorrow. And again, rain. They could have been shooting in Rio today, but flexibility is not these people's trump card. I feel my life wasting away in this dull hotel, incarcerated forever until the rain clears. In the lobby all the crew are waiting dutifully to go out after the downpour. Jules, the Polish/Brazilian producer, black leather jacket nipping in his narrow waist, parchment complexion, paces around frantically in control. Gripping his walky talky like a baby's bottle he discusses endlessly satellite forecasts. Paul Mazursky relied on them heavily and they were mostly accurate, he spouts. But in our case the rain is steadily pissing

down, defying the forecast, even if it was inclined to be more
obedient to the other film.

Robert Mann wafts up and now says, 'They're discussing
whether to go back to Rio' – which has been my contention
for days. The crew is demoralised by sitting around. Everybody is bored, frustrated or pissed, and Paul Freeman is busy
arranging parties. I am getting angry at the sheer waste. We
are no more than three hours from Rio. Travel at night and
be ready to work in the morning – since I am dying to tear
more pages off this script.

The director and his woman are now indissoluble and face
each other all day, as the film takes on the aspect of a Buñel
plot. We're all trapped and unable to leave. She is the devoted
lady, always at hand, and you feel that in her devotion she
would lay down her life for it. They are playing backgammon
and are thus spared the necessity of facing the anguished
expressions of the world outside. They protect each other
and turn inwards. Every time I pass this little alcove, which
is a kind of games room, I see them bent down in silent
concentration. Since they face each other they are immune
to the accusations of the hostile world that fails to recognise
his genius. Sometimes it is very necessary to have your
woman with you, as a kind of comfort station to receive all
the shit you might otherwise fling all over the place. Also she
diffuses your frustration, anger, self-doubt, and she pours oil
over troubled waters and 'lives' for her man – the warrior
who goes out against all odds. I'd have been glad too to be
able to return to a friend; be soothed, have my brow caressed,
and be comforted at the gas station of life! Oil for smooth
running; petrol for energy; a good burn up now and then;
and a polish and a service. I approached the duo as they
were playing their endless game and almost gently suggested
that we return to Rio, since there at least we could work,
and the chances were that it could rain for a week.

Julia lifted her head up, although I was addressing the
director, and responded like she was defending the realm
from the German invasion and, in her laconic New York
voice, said 'If we leave now we're screwed', looking at me as

if this was sacred testament. 'We're screwed', she repeated, as if savouring this new authority, not suspecting that we're screwed now as we wait for days and do nothing and everybody gets gradually demoralised. Here we are not screwed.

Lech didn't look up but busied himself with the plastic pieces. 'We're screwed' rang in my ears. Not even a 'Yes, you may be right . . . Let's give it a few more hours . . . We have emergency plans . . . sorry you're kept hanging around . . . Be patient . . . we'll deal with it . . . have a drink . . . how are you?' No. 'We're screwed' . . . I suddenly felt that I dropped into the wrong party. I moved away and they congealed back into their silent game. The weekend crowd of the Rioccan middle classes were now streaming into the hotel and making lots of noise and determined to enjoy themselves, and fat little kids were suddenly rearing down corridors, thus adding to and compounding my sense of doom and isolation.

Paul introduced me to his American friends who were extraordinarily articulate, and the older man regaled us with a story of how a nuclear silo was built. He told it with such wit and information that I was both aghast and entertained. His views were modest and intelligent – as were his wife's – and I realised how little vital communication I have had in the past months. Except for my Gogol, which I read at all opportunities.

Friday

Mauro, Paul's driver, gets seedier and seedier, and starts to resemble a serf in *Dead Souls* . . . And he even acts like one: servile, smiling, running around and buying booze for his master, being sent out on errands. It must be good to have a serf. I must get one. No wonder the Brits found it hard to give up their colonies. . . .

The rain stopped.

11.20 a.m. on the set, watching our director in swim suit, revealing his sturdy Polish legs, framing his hands to form a

square like a camera lens. Wilke turns up and we talk and
compare literature – like ping pong, something that under-
employed people do . . . like comparing restaurants. Names
are thrown in the air and tossed backwards and forwards,
more for demonstrating how literate one is than for any
insightful and shrewd appraisal of the author. It's like 'Do I
know more than you?' But sometimes it has its benefits and
it's a way of revealing the things you like as a means of
identification. Thomas Hardy I didn't know; then Gogol,
which he knew quite well and likes as much as I do now . . .
through to Dostoyevsky, Dickens (he loves and I don't know
in the least), Shakespeare; and work through: Hemingway,
Melville (big fan) . . . and on to Burroughs, then Mailer's
Ancient Evenings (which I thought was a brilliant reconstruc-
tion), nipped over to Kafka, of course, and he sees himself
as Joseph K. – which I also did many years ago and always,
as usual, deprived myself of the performance by having to
direct it. So I played Titorelli as a wonderful cameo, when
my whole purpose in adapting that gargantuan labyrinth was
to express the spirit of Kafka via K. However I did play the
bug. Once. And on Wilke goes, rattling off the masters and
needing to be the centre of attention – which he is anyway
because of his marvellous and volatile energy.

Sunday 4 October: Yom Kippur!

Yesterday as usual on this spit of beach for which we have
journeyed for another needless day. We hang about a bit,
and then it rains and we all dash under the tent. Ate a steak
to fortify me against further immersion in the sea. It's Yom
Kippur, Wilke tells me. I sense a slight shock, loss and twinge
of guilt that I pay no attention to such things any more, when
once it meant something special in one's life.

Sunday 4 October, José Wilke's fight 10.15 a.m.

Back on the beach. Yesterday our Brazilian star, José Wilke,
like all of us on a cool drizzly day, had to get in the sea with

his clothes on . . . then wait shivering and wet for the cameras to roll. Jessel shouts, 'The actors are getting cold!' We
wrap towels around our wet shirts and wait.

Then we did the scene on my close-up three or four times;
then José's close-up . . . once . . . twice . . . and José putting
his all into it. Then the director decides I should really be
standing. Was I standing? – he asks. While we shiver and
shake. He decides I was at that stage, which makes the last
two wet takes worthless. So much for continuity. Was I
standing? Nobody's too sure; so I stand. José blows a fuse
and launches into an explosive, but controlled, rage about
the sheer lack of professionalism on this film. The stupidity
of asking him, an actor, about continuity, while we freeze
and sicken.

He was of course right in this instance, even if his own
professionalism could be called to task. Anyway such decisions should be made before we put our guts on the line.
José's face burned like a torch. His black eyes blazed and it
was a performance of manic power and awesome to behold.
I wished there were opportunities in this fearful script for
explosions like this. It ignited the frustration which had been
building up like a powder keg inside him. Portuguese never
sounded so powerful and rich. It had the smell of Greek
tragedy. His rage was clean and centred and it scorched
through all the vagueness and sloppiness of the proceedings.
It was an astounding delivery, and José – wet in his black
pants and vest, his hair plastered back – looked like a sleek
black rat, his sharp nose flaring and white and his teeth
bared. All in Portuguese; and from the guts where this man
lives.

The director, as usual, sounded hopeless in the face of
this purging onslaught. He becomes confrontational in such
situations, as if not to lose face. 'We need it for continuity . . .
Let's do the fucking scene.' Reverting now to English and
sounding no less ferocious, José continued. 'Continuity!' he
howled. 'Is that *my* job? . . . Mine is acting . . . it's your job!'
His outburst was an act of purging himself of contamination
– such as I had done some weeks earlier. When the scum

builds up you have to vomit it out or make yourself ill. The poison must escape. The endless hanging about and the diminution of his talent! José wants to be happy – to enjoy his work, to express himself. Here was a typical contrast in the clashing of personalities. The heavier, stoic Polish temperament and its legacy of bureaucratic domination, and the Brazilian temperament which was inflammable and dedicated to the fulfilment of pleasure – in talk, work, food, music, bacchanalia and carnival.

It was always a clash between this mercurial José and the oppressive atmosphere on the set. During his tirade the set became deathly quiet. Every heart was beating for him. All the unspoken thoughts were being expressed by him. Isn't that what drama is about? To vicariously have your fantasies and hopes expressed for you? His voice was deep and the anger continued. No screaming, and no breaking of voice. Just a steady stream of raging heat. Splendid performance – and everybody enjoyed it immensely. He was a wild black panther that had been tormented too much.

Now a curious thing happened when the volcano had subsided: people started to move to José's chair on the beach where he now sat, still steaming but quiet. Everybody – and I mean the Brazilians – seemed to gravitate to him, as if he had touched something and had become a sacrifice. They offered him brandy and coffee; they wanted to be near the power or the source of it. Even I moved to him, as if terribly attracted to the performance, and wished to offer libations, comfort, cigarettes. It was curious that he was considered the wounded one, the brave one.

[After, in the hotel, José rang me to apologise for his behaviour, since he thought he had disgraced himself in front of his British friend. At which I assured him he most certainly had not, but the reverse – that he had given one great performance and I wished we could have filmed it. Somewhat mollified, he thanked me, and buried his mouth in a telephone for the next hour as he tried to get through to Rio, which seems an impossible task here.]

Still, the director has a difficult task, with his army of

clowns as he goes from place to place shouting JESS*eeee*L – in the way a baby shouts '*Mamaaaaaa!*' – and Lech resembles a giant baby sometimes, in his little blue swim suit and squat stocky legs. And poor thin assless Jessel rushes to obey, and does his job well, skilfully and with humour. Never have I seen a better and more patient and dedicated first assistant. Without Jessel I am sure this film in these circumstances could not have been made.

The steaks arrived for lunch at 3 p.m. and we don't seem to have got very far. I spend a lot of time staring at the sea, hearing 'JESS*eeee*L' in the distance – which now seems like the cry some birds make from time to time with no apparent reason but just to exercise their throats. I compare the giant boulders on the beach to Gargantua's loaves, all smooth and rounded. After his row yesterday José didn't turn up for today's shooting. Quite brave of him in one sense, but he has almost finished his rôle; and they dress up an extra and shoot from behind.

Back in the hotel the evening drags on, and I think I'm going gradually mad with only my *Dead Souls* to keep me alive and stop my mind from registering 'tilt'. Even a small chat with Paul Freeman's young Californian friend becomes confrontational. We talk about make-up, and suddenly I become obsessed by the idea that all women who wear lipstick are terminally insane. I can't believe that normal people paint their lips, and then keep painting them all through the day, as if their lives depended on it. Suddenly, in this wilderness, my civilised veneer is wearing off and my loneliness peels away anything fakey; but it also makes me extremely intolerant. As I watch millions of women shove this red grease all over their mouths, I think of the billions of dollars thrown away while the poor starve in their shanty towns. All that money's kept out of the stomachs of the hungry. Well it makes sense to me, and I can't see why others don't agree. This particular lady must have thought I was slightly batty and said, 'My friends might think I was ill if I didn't wear any.' Probably no one in her life had ever asked her a question like why she wore make-up.

Why do I get so involved? Sometimes I think I must have been dropped from another planet, so ridiculous seem human habits to me. One gets used to all things as being normal through conditioning, so I surmise that the strain of this work is loosening up that conditioning in me. Isolation and drugs have the same effect. Once, many years ago, someone gave me a very powerful drug. I only took it once but it altered my perceptions so much that I found that everybody around me was talking trivial unadulterated shit, and that the real important values were hunger and thirst, warmth and comfort; touch. Chatting about movies and other trite comments were a product of conditioning. I had a touch of that here. But more likely I was heavily laying down my frustration at the poor girl's feet.

5 October

Had strange dreams about Laurence Olivier, whose signature bears a slight resemblance to mine. Perhaps he is invading my body. In my dream Ken Tynan was criticising his acting, saying he didn't always reach the back because his tones were 'blaggy' . . . I suppose meaning puffy or boomy. I fiercely defended Sir L., saying that even when he whispered it was delivered with such ferocity that you heard every word – and I demonstrated it to him. Sir and Joan seemed pleased with my whole-hearted defence and, as Sir L. was on the way to the Savoy for an event, I offered to drive him in the Jag. When I reached my Jag it had shrunk from a large XJ12 to a small sports. Sir L. said it was a trifle small and could he rest his feet on the dashboard? I pulled the hood down, although this was certainly not my car – yet in dreams one hopes that it will somehow turn into the nice big Jag in which I wish to escort Sir L. I fastened down the hood and, when I looked, it was an old 1920s Jag. I panicked, knowing Sir L. would be late and there was now a rush hour and no way of getting a cab. End of dream.

The last day here at Angra, and it will be a long one on the beach. All one can hope for is an end to this torture.

Every scene that is written is shot . . . nothing is cut. Every little turd is preserved; nothing elliptical; we see everything from ABCD. No chance to jump and use our imaginations. When we are in a night club we have to be seen arriving in a car and getting out. When Biggs sells T-shirts we have to see him clutching them under his arm . . . like a beach vendor at Copacabana. Everything kept except what really matters – and that is the spirit of Biggs. And that is no fault of the excellent P. Freeman. The script is such a fiction of his life, and when Ronny told it to me I was enthralled, both by the telling and the story. 'Not enough movement' said the producers . . .' Need to pep it up.'

I don't know if I can take one more day on this beach, hearing the director shouting 'JESS*eeeee*L'. Even the tropical paradise of the beach has become the worst of nightmares.

10.15 a.m. Guilt:

I can sometimes endure my suffering, since I know that it can be turned into a creative expression – which is a way of relieving the suffering and you make your pearl. In fact my pain has been responsible for some of my most powerful works. *Kvetch* now runs 18 months in the U.S.A. – a play hewed out of every pain I ever felt. Every angst that gnawed away inside I put outside – and how people laughed. It shows us that things kept within fester and thrive, which outside can hardly keep alive.

This journal starts to bother me since I feel the need to censor myself. Something written in the heat of the moment stays in print forever. Why fear to write what's in your heart? And yet it is better sometimes to just grip it and suffer silently and handle the thing, than to winge at every shadow – fly to your journal and whine into it, like burying yourself in Mum's aprons. Then later to sell it and cause pain and discomfort in others. However one can't censor ones thoughts or feelings – just refine the end-product or put it in other ways.

On the film unit people after a while seek after their own kind and split off into little groups with common themes. At such times it is not unusual to find me alone. Very alone. And this week, in this remote place of Angra, is one of them. There's only three Brits, so there's not much choice: you take it or leave it. In this I seem not to be the one that's left, and so it's not hard to cultivate and get to know the Brazilians. During my depression I hardly noticed them and was very inward – protected as I was by my mate – but now I have to make an effort or stew in my own juices, which are very acidic. The Brazilians are very open and easy to get to know. It must be a nightmare to be on a very long location shoot . . . with few of you . . . and to find you have very little to relate to. Murder . . . hostility and isolation. It must be hell. No wonder actors usually bring their wives or girl friends . . . At least you're guaranteed one sympathetic and friendly face.

Always guilt. After two dunkings in the boat, and several runs along the beach, Hans Flury brought the press to view the proceedings and interview the cast; which is a trifle dangerous I would have thought. Naturally I spew my load – which wasn't really so bad – like, I can't wait to finish etc. And the reporter turns out to be a Brit living in Rio who had seen me in *Decadence* and was puzzled as to what or why I was doing this. I feel I still owe some loyalty to who pays me, and I tone down the horror. It has been painful and demoralising – but don't feel guilt over everything you express or write or you will be a head case. Sometimes you have to say it. I feel like a stooly. Just leave it now. Another day in hell . . . Hell is yourself . . . Just relax for now. So tired. So worn out with my life . . . my guilts . . . Just want peace and friends. Just watching *Black Orpheus* with his wife and at permanent peace fills me with envy. The view and the place are beautiful. Bite it!

6 October

Reading Gogol tells me more about myself and the human condition than anything I've read for years. Sometimes I feel I'm reading about myself when he writes so brilliantly about leading the 'noiseless life'. This book *Dead Souls* can actually lift you away from your despondency by showing you where you are. You identify with the cankered hero in some aspects, and then leap away from the revulsion he instils. The character acts as a map of human greedy ambition; or even as a diagnosis of disease. His small-mindedness is the hole through which he plummets. You read and diagnose your own failings by placing yourself in the situation. Never be an ass-licking slob and always be in command of yourself . . . The poor hero is always depending on the goodwill of others. What a feast of images float before my eyes . . . Must read more. This is what I gained from being *alone*! My discovery of Gogol . . . in Angra dos Reis.

Yesterday performed some of the mindless drivel that is so necessary for the edification of the lower orders who react only to what is familiar to them . . . Running along the rocks . . . Peeping from behind them . . . The police chasing me and running past the camera. All good stuff. Running the other way . . . flattening myself against a wall . . . The police tear past again. Images of Keystone Cops.

This film makes me feel like a young schoolboy that has been demoted from a high grade to a low one. This feeling was never so strong as when I was transferred from my grammar school in the East End to one in Hackney – made necessary by the move from our slum in Anthony Street E.1 to a new council flat, still stinking of paint, in the grim lands of Manor House, N.4. For some stupid reason the headmaster saw fit to place me in a 'C' stream, although I had been in an 'A' stream at the famous Raines Foundation School. I was unbelievably depressed and tearful, and remember going home that lunchtime with a fearfully heavy heart. After that demotion I couldn't care less, and no longer took any interest in school. Children must feel that their talents are recognised and rewarded. What idiot did this to me, when I was a bright spark – with my proud, high-scoring end-of-term reports? I don't think I fully recovered, and went rapidly on a downward lunge which eventually led to juvenile courts. And I can trace it from that first lunch time when I crossed Hackney Downs with tears in my eyes and feeling like a stupid shit.

I was reminded of this in this film. I was down-graded to the 'C' group and felt equally humiliated – and felt a slob more times than I care to remember. Whereas when I was at the Wyndhams with *Decadence* – or at the Mermaid Theatre – I was in the 'A' grade. Here my spirits have sagged, and I have become a rather timid, depressed, crushed orphan, ticking the days off to freedom.

11.56 a.m.

Back on the beach. Again we sink the boat; and this time it works. There's a miserable look at breakfast. Everyone badly wants to go home. P. Firth stalwartly refuses to do scenes that he feels are unnecessary, or repeat endlessly the same shots. He puts the ultimatum, and I admire his tenacity. With his cherubic looks and blonde curls, he has a steely centre. We all agree we've had enough. The film has been extended each week, until now we are three weeks over schedule – which under normal conditions might have been pleasurable. So there's a mini revolt going on. It has to stop on the 11th October. The actors are all stranded in the web of the film, entangled and unable to extricate themselves, weighing up in their minds what their limits are – of boredom, disappointment and longing for home. We have been here now on the beach for one week.

At night I'm in my hotel room after two *caiperenas*, wondering what everyone else is doing; watching *Raiders of the Lost Ark* for the second time, since P.F. is in it, and being far less impressed by the second showing, since 'effects' wear out much quicker than brilliant acting. You can watch great acting many times, but a roomful of hissing snakes is just a roomful of hissing snakes.

Suddenly, flying through my window, is this brown beetle that whacks its wings against the wall, sounding like a giant lawn mower. I loathe them – as soon as I open my window they aim for the light. They're like tough hazel nuts. I gingerly wrap a towel around this one and prise it off the floor and then shake the towel over the balcony. But they stick to the towel like burrs. Eventually I throw the whole towel downstairs where it lands on the pavement. There is a growing number of towels out there. My large fruit basket courtesy of the hotel and given to all guests is now a den of flies. My environment is resembling Polanski's *Repulsion* . . . I go to bed and read, and hear the beasts cracking their skulls against the window.

3 p.m.

Since we are trying to make this the last day here we are moving at speed. Captain Bligh is screaming at those who had the temerity to eat lunch. 'We have to finish today or we come back tomorrow' he threatens. The people eating their cooling lunches weren't working at the time, so it seemed quite normal to eat. They were shooting at the other end of the beach and, when the location shifted, a small group of hungry workers were found guiltily scoffing down their food; including me. So I ate my lunchtime steak. Too much meat is clogging up my system, but that's all they bring here – or those awful smelling, ubiquitous beans.

Pete Firth confesses that he categorically refuses to go beyond Sunday! Such a relief to find an ally in suffering when I thought I was the only one that hated what I was doing – not so much the acting, which could afford the rare respite, but the endless takes which grind you down to powder and you no longer recognise yourself.

It's a beautiful day and not too hot and the sea was soft and warm. The shrill piping of the birds runs through the woods, and I saw a giant leaf insect flying through the air – the size of a sparrow. Small beetles, looking in flight like butterflies, land on you with their striped yellow and black wings.

Thursday 8 October: Back in Rio!

Drove back yesterday morning after a huge thunderstorm that tore out of the sky like an avalanche hurtling down pieces of ice from God knows where. I had seen nothing like it. The sand outside my window looked as if it were being sprayed with machine gun fire. So had to stay another night in Angra – which pissed me off since I was so looking forward to leaving after work. But no driver would take me; not in that weather, even after it had subsided. I begged Paul Freeman's driver, but he looked deranged and wild-eyed, as if there were demons out there; but also he was far too loyal to his master.

So after dinner I watched the hideous, sloppy *Flashdance* on the cable. The cute heroine with her evil temper who wants to 'make it' as a dancer, and goes to confession to show how wholesome she is – when really she represents the new American harpie, the Maenad, the disgusting self-centred child-woman with whom we are all supposed to identify; a picture of neurotic ambition.

Back for the last week of this mess. Rebellion in the camp, since not only has the picture gone on for 13 weeks – which is longer than it took to shoot Speilberg's *Raiders* – but now they want even *more* days. It's over. All refuse to take the train on its long meandering journey to Palookaville any longer. The tiny set-ups and unambitious shooting schedule – and endless takes – have proven to be the film's undoing. And now they are having to pay for this indulgence. Unfortunately there was no strong guiding hand to say 'No!' – until Hans Fleury flew in from Switzerland to try and salvage it. The long days with no end . . . Scenes that were a morning's work, stretched into two days. Perhaps the results will show a creative mind at work and the film to be a masterpiece – since pain is no guarantee of a bad picture. It could be that the suffering will be redeemed by the end product. Lech is creative and his cameraman a long-suffering experimenter. Who knows?

Rushing through the last shots like for an episode of

EastEnders. Two or three takes and that's it! Still L. Asks for
another position and P. Firth flatly refuses. 'You've done it',
he says. 'It's finished. Three times we did it and that's it.'
Lech protests that he only has one good take. We all view it
on the video and it looks perfectly good. 'Lech', Peter says
– very firmly and without blowing a gasket – 'Let's get on
with it. We've got little time left' Since that last and final day
is Sunday and no one is staying further Pete adds. 'You have
little time left. Let's finish the film.' 'So you won't do it?'
Lech responds rather resignedly. 'No', Peter says, 'It's done.
We can't keep shooting scenes in two places to see which
looks better.'

I admire P's forthrightness. I might have endured it all
until it burst out of me like a volcano. Peter and Paul both
have firm and very diplomatic ways of dealing with this
situation. So Firth deals with it while I am released from it.
Firth takes on the attitude of a leading actor who is not used
to being treated or used in this fashion and makes this clear.
Whereas, since I had to carve out any opportunities for
work myself, I became used to overtly hostile criticism and
therefore reacted strongly to imposition and authority. I had
become like a whipped dog that won't react until the pressure
gets too great, and then I might bite. Over the years I had
received positive and negative criticism for trying to make
gainful employment, but the negative criticism had, in recent
times, become more starkly prejudiced and more vicious. It
astounded me to receive damaging reviews when I thought
I was trying to create a vital theatre. I would have thought
that critics might have said 'Thank God for some new life
at least.' So I had developed a hardened skin . . . until the
pain becomes too extreme. Whereas Firth sounds the warning note early on.

Friday 9 October

We all signal to each other, mouthing the word 'three', or
holding up three fingers to solidify our aims and the joy that
the small number 3 means to us. The film inevitably rolls to

its end, and we are working speedily and squeezing the story
into the canisters of film which we have used at a vast rate.
It feels as if there is life after *Prisoner of Rio*. The director is
working like a man who knows that his power over us will
soon end and is grabbing all he can, while he can. Nobody
will be sorry – except perhaps Lech, and his constant com-
panion, who watches his every take, glued to the video screen.
A loyal and steadfast mate watches the master's steps, probably inwardly wincing at each riposte of some rebelling
actor. It is a partnership that allows no intrusion; but it can
suffer from its exclusivity since the pain cannot be assuaged
by the actors, nor can a symbiosis be formed. Also there have
become two voices to appease, four eyes, four ears, rather
than two. As one shot looks good, the partner will suggest
something else . . . so the director will not be accessible to
the opinions of his peers or able lieutenants. No doubt her
presence is a comfort and necessary help – especially in this
situation with mixed crew and languages – and is a calming
one for the director. But I am used to directors working
alone and with able assistants. The emotional bonding, with
a wife or lover as No. 2, cuts you off from your team. That
is my opinion anyway, and I would never – if I was directing
a movie – have my wife on set as my assistant, since the crew
and cast see you as a God symbol creating order and purpose,
and 'Thou shalt have no other god but me'. It is also demean-
ing to the performer, since he feels his work is having a
second judgement cast on it. I suppose actors are jealous
creatures and like their director to be the boss, accountable
at all times to them for advice and help; and, in that tempor-
ary time of filming, to enter a family relationship. Perhaps
this is a simple-minded opinion of mine, but I would hesitate
if such circumstances were to arise in the future.

As the work draws to its final take, a great weight seems
to be lifting off. What once felt like shackles of iron are now
hardly felt at all. One starts to speak more easily about future
plans. What we are doing next is the familiar tune. Trips to
other parts of Brazil are contemplated. Even Rio, which once
seemed heavy and oppressive, now starts to grow attractive.

The sun shines regularly down, after weeks of rain, and the sea never looked so brilliantly clean and emerald green. Tastes are returning, and the nights are full of wonder. The *caiperenas* taste better than ever.

A welcome relief on this film has been the constant presence of a very sweet mulatto who is the coffee boy. Outrageously attired and audaciously camp, he swans around the set offering relieving libations of coffee, tea, apples, orange juice to the shock-worn troops, and always seems to appear when you need him most. As you sit in a heap of crumpled dejection a small soft voice will purr . . . 'Café Steve?' Just as you are flaking out in the heat he will arrive with a huge basket of sliced melon. With his broken front tooth, his cracked smile, and the funny hat he always wears, he takes on the character of a Brazilian pixie. He has adopted a variation of English punk, with old tights and torn vests.

Roberto Mann – our Assistant to the director/ investor/ dogsbody/ and good ally – has an endearing habit of rubbing his nose thoughtfully, as if a genie will spring out of its curvaceous and oleagenous masses. It's a habit, he confesses, of his old, bad, coke days that leads observers to believe he still does it. But he doesn't; just rubs his nose and talks incessantly about the film. Roberto is a shrewd wheeler-dealer, and not only found a good portion of the investment, but acts as a whipping-block – as well as the other afore-mentioned duties. They all desperately want to see a return for their investment, and therefore do anything to oil the tracks until it reaches home. Roberto is always 'there' . . . ready to run, and usually stripped down to the waist. His scrawny, sinewy body looks like a battleground from several operations, yet active and strong. His child bride of nineteen is the obvious source of his joy since he lights up like a beacon whenever she appears on the set; and then she clings to him like a vine round a tree. And it's not hard to see why. He gives off an air of total enthusiasm for whoever he's with and takes no sides. He enthuses about all the sweeter aspects of living – like music, dance, booze, good food ('I know a special little place . . .') and adventure – and his dark eyes fire with enthusiasm. He tells us stories of his adventures in gold dealing in the Amazon when, illegally, he would buy gold from the miners who worked this gigantic hell hole in the middle of the Amazon forests. The miners each had a claim the size of a pocket handkerchief, and worked it until they dropped dead from exhaustion, or made a lucky strike. They'd go up and down spindly ladders as the pit grew deeper, carrying the waste and rocks to the surface where it is then crudely filtered for gold. Each man has to carry 100lb sacks on his shoulders, and makes the journey at least thirty times a day – up these steep, ricket ladders. It is a life belonging to the nightmares of Hieronimous Bosch – a giant ant-heap of moving flesh. How to earn a living. This film isn't so bad after all!

Saturday 10 October

Two days. left. It starts to crawl, and vague, half-hearted efforts are made to do something together to celebrate the last days and the total achievement of actually filming this heap of script. But nobody is much interested in doing anything special . . . no wrap party for the workers; no celebration for our sweat; no thank you for going through hell. We should at least have a farewell feast with Biggs, but I am reluctant to suggest anything. Everything seems an effort, as if we are hanging on and dribbling out our last remaining drops of enthusiasm for the work before ceasing to be. I realised that we are not linked together by anything more than the necessity of working together. This is more than a shame. I almost want to force it on us! Today is Saturday. The last day to do it, since Firth leaves tomorrow. The three of us have sweated, suffered, tortured ourselves – and put up with sheer unmitigated and unrelenting boredom. Sounds like what I hear about the National Theatre for the small part players.

'The truck is on fire . . . You look at the window . . . See that Biggs is missing and run past the camera . . .' Since this takes place in a public park, a crowd of people have gathered to watch this piece of nonsense – as people do when they see a camera on location. I feel like a prize jerk. 'How all occasions do inform against me'. I run, like a piece of animated rubbish, past the lens. Nothing means anything any more . . . my personality in shreds . . . my ego in the toilet. Just me in the same stupid tie I have worn for three months running past the camera. I am ashamed for some reason that people are watching us, and at the silliness of some of the things you have to do. The sheer drivel of most films casts you into the slough of despondency, but to have the public witness your humiliation adds vinegar to the wounds. I call to Jessel, 'Clear the crowd Jessel, they're in my eyeline' – as if this matters. But I don't want them there, happy and relaxed, watching me trying to run. Perhaps I should never do film again with its need for mindless running around engaging in trivial activities. How many films are *On the Waterfront*? And why was it so successful? Because its actors had a chance to let rip on the most interesting, human, succinct dialogue. Still, film pays the way, and you suffer in silence since you are paid suffering money. I see movie actors destroy themselves through drink and boredom, while the crummiest theatre engages the grey matter more than a multitude of crappy films. Mind you, the cameraman George keeps my spirits involved by telling me how marvellous it all looks. But I can only see it from the P.O.V. of an actor.

I knew it would happen. They crawl up to my car and beg me to do yet another day. Made the huge mistake of talking about a vacation in Brazil when this is over, so they know I don't have to rush back. And now my better nature is aroused, even if I have already given my pound of flesh. I've had enough; but curiously another day doesn't bother me that much. The torture is more or less over. It no longer touches me, except for the silliness of my actions. I saw Brazil. I earned some wages (no fortune). I wrote a journal, and met and like Ronnie Biggs. And I avoided my fiftieth birthday trauma in the U.K. But I politely refused another day. It could go on and on and . . . on.

Ultimo Day
October 11

Firth had not reneged on his ultimatum: 'Leave at 6 p.m. I'm getting on the plane, finished or not.' This seems to drive them into activity. Things are achieved. Hans Fleury adds weight to the statement that we must finish. 'Sunday is the last day and there is no more money!' Result: speed, activity. Result: less wastage. The more people are indulged, the more they waste. The more accommodating, the more exploited. The more decent, the more abused. In the end the film goes through a series of confrontations as it creeps forward.

The last day is beautiful, clear and fresh, and we are all called early – which is really symbolic since nobody is ready to start work. We're in a delightfully shaded park, which is itself set in the wooded slope of the Cocorvado. And in the distance you can see the stone Jesus swirled in a mist, as if ascending. In the centre of this park is a country mansion built in stone and marble, in the style of an eighteenth-century Italian palazzo. It was actually built for an opera singer by her Brazilian boyfriend; but she got bored after a while, missed Italy desperately, and went home. It's a perfectly shaped building which you enter up a flight of stairs which take you into the courtyard with a large, sunken pool in the centre. The pool is now a dried up and cracked space. The ceilings are embossed with small flowers and gilded. The walls are faced in matching marble panels – where the marble has been sliced in two the mirror opposites face each other, like two halves of a pear. It's now used as an art school, and the crappy useless sludge of modernism aches like a bad tooth in a beautiful face. The puerile expressions of the students are hung on the walls like a smack in the gob to the beautiful marble behind it.

We snack at the mobile canteen, and I see Mark Slater for the last time, wearing his money-belt and always appearing to be on top of it – although I believe his over-lenient schedule is the reason for our rush now. Whole nights spent wearily shooting a half page – like students. It was painfully slow, and now, of course, there is a panic. So now everybody comes to work. We shake hands and kiss. The ultimo diaz. Who cares that we all pile into one car? We used to have one car each, since we were needed at different times and cars are cheap enough here. But today it doesn't matter. No trailer either. We have been stripped.

Paul has his *Cuíca* – his drum with the stick which makes such a haunting sound, a kind of wheezing laughter. He's become very adept at it and I can just see him in his splendid house in the country on a wet Sunday afternoon, pulling on his *Cuíca* and evoking memories of a hot night in Brazil at the Escola de Samba . . . a thousand pulsing bodies, and the smoke rising from the spiced barbecue sticks outside the dance hall; the strong *caiperena* with its crushed limes and ice, and the fierce attacking *batteria* – an explosion of passion, a symbol of the heart beat; the rhythm of hip ignited by the drums. So he will sit there, gazing at the wet English country, producing sweet memories as he pulls on the string, like a genie out of a magic lamp. He may decide to wander down to his local, and hear the sounds of the fruit machine punctuating the limp evening air, and the stirring sounds of 'Time please' Macumba!

We were called at 7.30 a.m. and, an hour later, I am quite happy to be writing, sitting on the stone seats by the stone table in the park. Black Orpheus is playing cards with his wife. He is never away from her side – not for a second; and they lean on each other as if it was the most natural thing on earth to be part of each other's existence. Such devotion and dependence is very moving. He still has the gentleness and innocence of childhood – hence his youthfulness and vitality. Ten children have been sired by him, and he talks of having even more! He likes fooling around, the way men sometimes do when there are a lot of other men around. He pretends to slog me with a hugh pile driver, like in the old westerns – especially if I am unprepared. I feel a tap on my shoulder, I turn . . . and whack . . . he got me . . . and giggles his head off. I have to pay him back and, when I do, he obligingly 'reacts'.

Now it's nearly over everyone is at peace with each other. Mark no longer seems the threatening ogre in the office, but a rather overworked slave. Even Lech is smiling and cracking jokes. Once everyone has got what they wanted it's amazing the transformation that takes place. I have my freedom, plus my wages. Lech has his film. The actors go away satisfied and chock full of experiences. All are in some way satisfied, relieved, exhausted, and fulfilled. Now the pain is nearly over one can have the leisure to reflect on the time one has spent here, and catalogue the good times and reject the others. Only, who has paid for all this? The investors – who are yet to be satisfied; who are still waiting for the months of post-production – endless hours of post-synching, music, editing. And they still have to try to sell the thing. Ah! There's the rub. Will they see a return for their three million bucks? A lot of money for Brazil. Who knows the future of this film? Will we all be sitting in the Odeon, Leicester Square, sweating in shame?

Finishing Gogol's *Dead Souls*, and it's moved me and stimulated a whole nest of worms. The depth of his emotions casts a giant spotlight on my own, and made me scrutinise any action of mine that had some taint in it and cast it out. Reading of his characters' petty manipulations I suddenly identified with the trashiness of human actions that are furtive and guileful.

3.30 p.m.

Peter Firth has suddenly gone! Irrevocably and utterly gone. Out of our lives. His hotel room of three months, just a dead space with unmade bed; full of memories and old razors in the bathroom. Gone. Yet I see him on the Cocorvado in his Panama hat, squinting his eyes against the sun and uttering the dire words with a good grace and wit. Also by the pool in Paraguy; or being pulled out of a car umpteen times in Copacabana. Gone. Just a memory. He will shortly be on the

plane to New York and revelling in all the dreams and
fantasies of that enchanted and weird city. Just Paul and I
now.

I have at last torn out the last pages of this script. The
nightmare will soon be over, but will be stretched out to the
bitter end I have no doubt. But I will take joy in the last
moments. All the doubts, fears, future plans suddenly loom
up. All the little knots of ones life suddenly appear, needing
untangling. The film had provided a kind of desperate escape
from life and become a trial in itself. Now one has been
acquitted the jubilation will give way to trivial concerns: the
small aches and pains of life; the future plans; questions to
be answered. Everything rushes at you. Even this pain was a
camouflage against all others. 'Why did you do it?' Lech asks,
when I complain about the sheer, unrelenting banality of the
text. Could I say I needed an escape? Brazil offered that: an
escape from my life and the awesome dread of my fiftieth,
looming up like a giant line that you draw with a ruler under
a set of figures that you then add up. All other years are
bonuses. Here I fled into an unknown world and spent my
time being wrapped up in film like some plastic mummy;
staying awake all night and waiting to be called to march up
and down shouting 'Rita'. I bit on my humiliation, and one
night I reached the age of fifty during the shooting of a
scene; and did actually feel that from midnight – when the
shadow of the half century moved over me – I would lack
the bite I had before the fateful hour struck. My stage work
never felt so sharp and clear – but then I was still in my
forties! Then my birthday on the beach in Grumari under a
leaden grey sky – but warm, and the *caiperenas* softening the
blow, and the fish tasting so good in the open air where the
sea was smashing itself against the rocks – and it all felt
good.

In this park the birds are singing fiercely as twilight slowly
drains the day away and I can just about see the page in
front of me. Paul Freeman is inside and hurling flaming
towels out of the window to make good his escape. There is
a whiff of excitement in the air, and some really cheap, sour

wine is being handed out. I have two more scenes left, and
one of them with Paul; the last an interior. The end should
be an explosion, and a party will be held in the palace built
for the singer. We have all been handed our *Prisoner of Rio*
T-shirts, and have eaten the last rice and beans we will ever
eat. The sky is darkening, but still light enough for me to
see the silhouetted leaves cut out against the pale lavender
twilight.

Since losing our trailers – which insulated us against the
noise, stink, pollution and madness outside – we are now
forced to seek sanctuary in the bus. I even try to take a nap,
but the toing and froing of bodies makes this impossible; and
now there is a long queue in the bus for the cheques being
made to the workers who are rightly arguing about their
overtime.

Earlier I had a scene in the park where I slug a cop and
make good my escape. I had to start from a certain point so
the camera could catch me tearing round the corner. I wait
for action, and mark my starting point with a few leaves . . .
and saw under a leaf a miracle of creation: a cocoon just
hanging there, attached to a few threads. One of the most
astonishing events in nature was taking place. It looked full
of life and expectant. I could not take my eyes off it . . . such
a fine, vulnerable cocoon. A growth. A metamorphosis. Just
down the path, the unmentionable refuse of the human mind
was being spewed out. Think what miracles the human brain
is capable of: the unceasing wonder of its complex thoughts;
its senses that are capable of being amazed, enchanted, and
moved beyond imagination. And all translated into words, as
if words themselves were holy when put into a certain order
of things. I thought that for centuries words that found
themselves in print carried the most important messages and
ideas. Drama was written in verse, and shaped and spun to
carry the most secret thoughts on human experience. With
the invention of presses and mass manufacture, paper now
records the spittle of the Neanderthal brain – its gruesome
banalities. When paper was rare, and parchment laborious to

make, you could not, with your quill and ink, defile the white and precious space.

13 October

The last night was to be drawn out to the bitter end. The crew were determined *not* to work beyond midnight (only a sixteen hour day) – can you imagine this in England! But Lech was determined to go beyond. All the hesitations, over-shooting, and endless takes over the past three months gathered momentum in the last week – like a huge boil, full of the poisons of bad living, that must now be lanced. The backlog of work to be done fell on the backs of the workers, and the film was becoming a symbol of colonial imposition. The overwhelming hierarchy of 'Art' . . . Art comes first . . . How can you ever question it? It was obedience. I was told we would probably be doing an eighteen hour day: the evil fruit of slackness and indulgence. Jessel says, 'I'm only putting up with this for the sake of the film' – and that means the labour of 50 Brazilians, who are inexorably tied together. The very shirt that has been pressed and the crummy suit that has been cleaned umpteen times; even the sweet young boy with his coffee and fruit; the driver who takes us to the set; Conceptua, the make-up lady – who had hardly anything to do except spray water for sweat on my face – and the endless hours of boredom, relieved for her only by eating; the sympathetic 'Dada' who stroked my head sometimes, and always prepared my clothes – and was as sick to death of the one costume as I was as I stepped into the dreary uniform of my bondage; Mark, the 'soundman', who needed constant 'wildtracks' and 'atmosphere' – who was never satisfied and whose standards were never attained, yet fought to have his sound engineered as he wished since sound was his pride and joy; Jaques, who pulled focus, and whose ears heard the constant refrain, 'Was it in focus?' and who vaguely and unconvincingly replied, 'Sure it was' – who taught me the foulest words in Portuguese so I might secretly arm myself, since cursing has a way of discharging bile; whose signature was '*mais pornietta!*' when we got tired of too many takes. I remember the thousand times he would hold the tape up to my nose, always checking, and still managing to get it out of focus ... for George Moradian, the lighting/cameraman, whose one eye was always open as he stared through the lens with the other; always watching, until a red ring formed around his pupil – and I couldn't endure it, his symbolic marriage to his magic crystal; his quiet, patient voice never rising, and always encouraging me to go further – for all his hundreds of hours and 250,000 feet of film. 'Reloading' the familiar cry. We are forced to stop while a young woman carries in the new canisters of untouched film, like she was carrying in a new-born baby. For Danny, his younger brother, for creating light – for his patience and charming American ease ... For faces whose occupations and functions I was never sure of, but who would sometimes touch me on the shoulder the way Brazilians do and say '*Todo ben?*' – 'Everything O.K.?' For the slim, aesthetic looking man in charge of the video, who hardly ever spoke and never complained; who always worked stripped to the waist and never ate meat lunchtimes – and looked as if he didn't with his clean, strong face ... For Helmut Baptista who drove me through endless nights and softened the blow by teaching me erotic Portuguese as we spun round the endless traffic of Rio, heavy in heart on the way, and full of lightness returning ... For Ronnie Biggs for just being a totally big support, and loving to us all in a way that left you with no doubt about his feelings ... And for Flavia, in charge of transport and of sorting out the incredible complications of humans and machines ... For a driver of one of the trailers who, after an ugly explosion which cleared the air, rushed up with a cigarette and a beer to console me, as if he saw a wounded animal rather than a vindictive one ... who was always there to do something for the actors whenever they needed something, and whose child was cruelly taken from him by drowning, and yet turned up to work the following day, since he could not afford not to do so and felt he was needed. God bless him.

So when Jessel says he works for the film, then that is what he means: the collected will and energy of all his Brazilian workers – and not just the director and investors. And indeed we did work until 3.30 a.m. And in the courtyard of the palace I looked up and saw a pageant of stars, and the large round moon was sliding past the stone Christ high in the hill of Corcovado. A thin scarf of cloud was sliding down over the tips of the trees, and the air was balmy as silk. Rio looked truly beautiful from here and I was grateful to Lech for keeping us up, since when should I have the opportunity of seeing this dawn sight again?